Rolando Giustini has worked on a variety of motion pictures in Rome, Italy, at Cine Citta and Dino DeLaurentiis Studios and has written screenplays in Hollywood, where he has acquired much of his experience in the television field. Mr. Giustini teaches scripting, storyboarding, and cinema arts at the Art Institute of Pittsburgh and produces multimedia presentations for use in industry. He is also the author of a column for *Back Stage, New York,* the second largest filmmaking trade paper in the country.

THE FILMSCRIPT

A Writer's Guide

Rolando Giustini

A SPECTRUM BOOK

PRENTICE-HALL, INC., Englewood Cliffs, New Jersey 07632

Library of Congress cataloging in publication data

Giustini, Rolando.
  The filmscript.

  (A Spectrum Book)
  Includes index.
  1. Moving-picture authorship. I. Title.
PN1996.G48   808'.066791021   80-15090
ISBN 0-13-314252-3
ISBN 0-13-314245-0 (pbk.)

10 9 8 7 6 5 4 3 2 1

Printed in the United States of America

Editorial/production supervision and
interior design by Frank Moorman
Cover design by: Honi Werner
Manufacturing buyer: Barbara A. Frick

PRENTICE-HALL INTERNATIONAL, INC., *London*
PRENTICE-HALL OF AUSTRALIA PTY. LIMITED, *Sydney*
PRENTICE-HALL OF CANADA, LTD., *Toronto*
PRENTICE-HALL OF INDIA PRIVATE LIMITED, *New Delhi*
PRENTICE-HALL OF JAPAN, INC., *Tokyo*
PRENTICE-HALL OF SOUTHEAST ASIA PTE. LTD., *Singapore*
WHITEHALL BOOKS LIMITED, *Wellington, New Zealand*

CONTENTS

Introduction, vii

Chapter One
THE CONCEPT
1

Chapter Two
THE OUTLINE
7

Chapter Three
THE TREATMENT
17

Chapter Four
THE SCREENPLAY
29

Sample Master Scene Script
Night Flight
33

Chapter Five
THE SHOOTING SCRIPT
105

Sample Shooting Script
Night Flight
115

Chapter Six
STORYBOARDING
233

Index, 243

For mother and father who paved the way; my children, Jeanne and Roxanne, who shared me; Chris Sohl, "my main man," who hit the keys; and Rosanna, my loving wife, who is always there.

INTRODUCTION

INSTRUCTIONS
Please read

Another introduction apologizing for another book on a subject on which too many books have already been written? No! Just a few words on how this book should be used. This book is a guide for writers on the development of the filmscript.

But it is more. This book also provides a guide for the hyphenated filmmaker, one who serves more than a single function—writer-director as an example—or who serves as the total filmmaker, the *auteur* or author, acting as a combined producer-writer-director-cinematographer.

This book is unique for several reasons: First, it covers all stages of previsualization from concept through the various stages of development, outline, and treatment, to the various script forms such as the master scene and the shooting script. But we do not stop there; we include a final section on story-boarding—one important phase of previsualization which is ignored by most books. At the end of each section is a sample work, an actual example of the form we have been covering.

In this book we will work together on *one* project from beginning to end.

The importance of the script cannot be overemphasized. Generally a film is a collaborative effort which demands that many people and their work be coordinated. The script provides a standardized form for not only describing the action, but also for getting information to these people—a way of developing and transmitting all this information to all these people in one convenient package.

As I've stated, this book will be dealing with one film project which we will continue throughout the book. Therefore, let us proceed to the first step. The evolution of the script begins with the *concept*.

THE FILMSCRIPT

chapter 1

THE CONCEPT

PREVISUALIZATION

To previsualize literally means to "see before." That is exactly the purpose of script writing: to see the film before it is actually made.

Scripting is previsualization. In the script we try to see or predict how the film will look. The implication here is that we know how it should look. This means that the film exists in its entirety in the mind of the writer—it is a kind of cerebral cinema. The chart on the following page shows the steps of development that the writing goes through in its progress toward the final stages of previsualization.

At this point the film is a concept in the mind of the writer.

The importance of "seeing the film before" its production is to help draw up a shooting schedule and a budget for the financing of the film.

Sets are designed and constructed from the script. Actors and actresses develop their characters and obtain their lines from the script. Locations for shootings are chosen based on the script. Costumes are designed from details in the script, and special effects are the studio magician's way of bringing to life the fantasy and imagination the writer puts into the script.

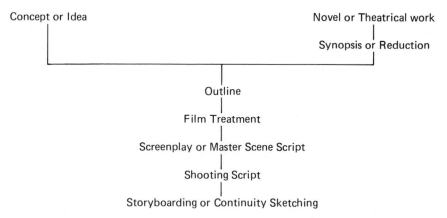

When a film is financed, millions of dollars are spent on something which does not yet exist, based entirely on the writer's words on those pieces of paper. Thus, a multimillion dollar industry is set into motion by the script.

IMPORTANCE OF A SCRIPT

In the production of motion pictures the importance of the script cannot be overemphasized.

Film is a collaborative art, and we have often heard from individuals in the various areas that "many bad films have been saved by the . . .," meaning editing, music, or whatever. This may be true, but there wouldn't even be any *bad* films to save without scripts. Excluding experimental films (in which previsualization may not be a part), all films must have a script.

Even members of the avant-garde cinema—Fellini, as an

example—whose names conjure up images of scriptless, improvisational film productions, rely heavily on the script.

In the early sixties in Rome, the wife of a friend of mine was working as a secretary for a new Fellini production. Through her efforts, I did a little work on a script for that film and also got a chance to act in it. The film was an ill-fated work called *The Voyage of G. Mastorna,* and was never completed because of legal problems between Fellini and his producer, Dino De Laurentiis.

My disappointment in the shelving of that production, which occurred even after the sets had been built, was great. I not only lost a chance to act in Fellini's film—I had been one of the lucky ones to be selected—but of course my involvement in the script also came to an end. However, none of that could compare to my previous disappointment at finding out that my idol, Fellini, used . . . I hate to say it . . . a script.

The script is important because it is the "blueprint of the film." This phrase is often used in a negative way, revealing an attitude which I have never understood. What sane person would attempt to build a house without a blueprint? A script serves the same function as a piece of music to be conducted or a play to be interpreted on the stage. The importance of Frank Lloyd Wright, Mozart, or Shakespeare in relationship to their works would never be questioned. Why then question the importance of script writers or their contributions to the films that they write?

SCHOOLS OF THOUGHT

There have always been differing schools of thought on the importance of the script to the film and on the type of script that should be written, whether ironclad or loose. Pudovkin—and those Russian filmmakers who placed the greatest significance on editing—maintained that the script was editing a priori, in other words, before the fact. These filmmakers believed in the ironclad script that was not to be veered from. Alfred Hitchcock exemplifies this viewpoint in modern filmmaking. Steven Spielberg, continuing along these lines, even storyboarded the entire script for *Close Encounters of the Third Kind.*

On the other hand, some Russian filmmakers believed that the filmscript should not be followed too closely during filming, but rather after filming. They thought that one should film without restrictions and then use the script to direct the editing of the footage.

The other group which adheres to this "post-filming" scripting is represented by the avant-garde cinema, which began in the postwar years—exemplified by avant-garde filmmakers like Fellini and, more accurately, by some of the offbeat experimental filmmakers.

Today most filmmakers are dead center between these two extremes. Today's scripts are written before the shooting is done and followed loosely as a guide. The scripts written today are of the *master scene* type, without camera directions or division by shots, so that the director—the person with creative control—will be free to improvise and to exert his or her directorial imperative.

The building blocks of a script or film are the shots. *Shots* are the "words" of filmic language. Every writer has these same words with which to make a personal filmic statement; how the writer puts them together constitutes style. That is what is done in the script. The content and context of the shots are treated in the scripts.

But whether the script is used before the filming as a guide for shooting or after the filming as a guide for editing, its importance is still evident.

The script is the set of instructions that comes in the box telling us how to assemble the film we want to make.

THE CONCEPT

All films begin with an idea or *concept,* a unifying thread that runs through the entire production. The concept is what the film is about and can be anything from an original thought to a book or play. Some films have even been made from songs.

Many times while writing one becomes sidetracked, wandering off on some tangent or getting lost in some subplot; one then loses sight of the main elements of the script's subject. Often a writer is too close to his or her work and that can obscure the vision. Having a good concept on file enables the writer to step back, as it were, and regain an overview of the whole.

Many times one sees a film and becomes puzzled because the film does not address the issues or deal with the problems that it pretends to. Generally speaking, this is a result of losing sight of the concept of the work while still paying lip service to it. (This is similar to a collapse of plot structure due to lack of adherence to outline. We deal with this problem in Chapter 2, "The Outline.")

In conclusion, let me repeat that for the filmmaker—and I use this term in the broadest sense to include the writer, director and/or the total filmmaker—the most important and difficult task is to maintain at all times an overview of the film as a whole. This is extremely difficult to do because of the fragmented view one generally has of the finished product: the film as a whole.

In the collaborative effort of filmmaking, having a clear, well-defined concept which capsulizes the meaning of the entire film enables a writer to rush into the script without losing the creative way.

We will now begin our project with the concept. For our film project, let's say we choose to write about mercenaries. Let's create a psychological study about a man who becomes a mercenary soldier.

Sample Concept

1. A film about mercenaries, showing how they also are victims of the wars in which they are involved.

2. A disillusioned young man, unable to find success, is attracted by violence and its traditional ties to the romantic view of adventure.

3. He becomes a mercenary, but the reality of killing and the horror of war lead him full circle back home to an appreciation of the real meaning of the commonplace and the everyday.

chapter 2

THE OUTLINE

OUTLINE
General description, plan, or summary

We are now ready to begin our project. The *outline* is an expansion of the concept; it is a framework built one unit at a time, a framework on which to hang the narrative which will be the treatment.

In the outline the concept is expanded to a numbered chronology of what takes place in the film. The outline is a list of narrative units, large bits of action in which we decide what steps we wish to use to take the story from the concept to its conclusion.

We must now develop the plot of the film and decide in what direction the story will develop. The vehicles we will use to convey the message in the concept include elements such as *characters, dialogue, locations and settings, visual and audio symbols,* and *devices.*

The outline is a synopsis of sorts which begins to sketch out the principal characters and, most importantly, begins to explain the plot or storyline.

7

The outline, it should be remembered, is the first form in which a script can be registered with the WRITERS GUILD OF AMERICA, a practice which every new writer should get in the habit of doing. Usually treatments or actual scripts are registered, but at times when you are pressed to submit an outline for consideration it is wise to register the outline. This registration establishes a date of completion of the author's work.

Information for registration and fees is available through:

Writers Guild of America
8955 Beverly Boulevard
Los Angeles, California 90048

The process of amplifying the outline proceeds in two general steps:

1. Questions and Answers
   a. Determine what questions are in the concept.
   b. Answer these questions and combine with the concept to form a rough outline.

2. Filling in the Gaps
   a. Fill in the missing elements.
   b. Combine this additional information with the rough outline to form the second-draft outline.

From here, you simply repeat this process of amplification until you are satisfied that the plot has run its logical course.

Do not underestimate the importance of the outline. By carefully performing this process of amplification, the writer develops a good framework that can be referred to during the rest of the writing. The outline establishes the perimeters beyond which the writer will not want to go, and within which he or she will have complete creative freedom. Nothing is as confining to the creative process as total freedom; without some limitations the creative muscles have nothing against which they can exert their energy.

All one has to do to understand the truth of the above is to sit at the typewriter with a blank sheet of paper and try to write a script from the top of your head. A few years ago I found myself in a rush situation writing a script for a major television series. To save time, I tried to bypass the preliminaries and jumped right into the writing of the script. I jumped right in and almost drowned. I had to backtrack and, albeit very quickly, work up a good outline before I was able to complete the process.

Let's take the concept as we wrote it in Chapter 1 and begin its development into the outline.

Concept

A film about mercenaries, showing how they also are victims of the wars in which they are involved.

A disillusioned young man, unable to find success, is attracted by violence and its traditional ties to the romantic view of adventure.

He becomes a mercenary, and the reality of killing, the horror of war, leads him full circle back home to an appreciation of the real meaning of the commonplace and the everyday.

In the concept certain words and phrases imply additional information by asking certain questions.

Let's see in the following chart what plot is hidden in the concept and how it unfolds in the outline.

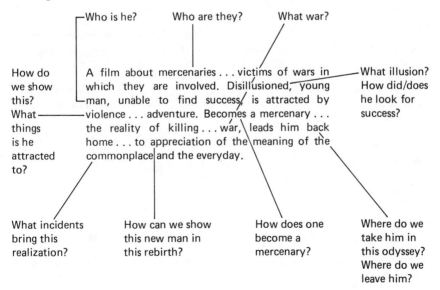

Our first expansion of plot will now happen when we answer these questions posed by the concept. The following example illustrates how this works.

Who are they? Let's give him a close friend who goes with him. His friend is Chuck.

Who is he? I am forced to start thinking in concrete terms. A name? OK. Let's call him Joe Bonner.

A film about mercenaries . . . victims of wars in which they are involved. Disillusioned, young man, unable to find success, is attracted by violence . . . adventure. Becomes a mercenary . . . the reality of killing . . . war, leads him back home . . . to appreciation of the meaning of the commonplace and the everyday.

Let's make him an intelligent man, possibly some college so that he can understand his situation. He can't find work and is bitter..

He loves guns, hunting, anything connected with guns. He lives vicariously through books and films, the adventures of others.

What war? Mercenaries used in Asia/Africa; it's contemporary.

How? My research tells me that many mercenaries simply answer ads in newspapers or magazines available on any newsstand.

Where do we leave him? He sees how wrong he was. After watching his friend die and almost losing his life, he runs home licking his wounds, to the monumental task of everyday life, survival, existence, and the commitment of love.

It's no fun anymore. He has to do his own killing face to face, not from the safety of the armchair or the theater seat.

Both when he reaches the States, and before, when he faces almost certain death, he begins to understand, to see the beauty of the simple things, the commonplace, and to miss them.

Now using these notes, the information which we saw between the lines in the concept, plus the original concept, we have a rough outline.

Rough Outline

1. A young man, Joe Bonner, can't find work after dropping out of college.

2. He lives alone surrounded by books and movie posters, all glorifying war, violence, and adventure, guns, knives, etc.

3. He and his closest friend, Chuck, decide to join an organization of mercenaries after seeing an ad in a magazine.

4. They go to Africa.

5. Joe, finally faced by real violence and death, realizes that war is a far cry from watching it in a comfortable theatre or reading about it in an adventure novel.

6. Joe and Chuck are cut off and are faced with what looks like certain death. Joe remembers small details of the now "not so bad" life back home. While waiting to die, they see the beauty in humble, simple things.

7. Chuck is mortally wounded and dies in Joe's arms. Joe succeeds in escaping.

8. Joe finally works his way back home to the States, realizing that real courage is in fighting the peaceful battles of everyday existence.

Taking this rough outline we fill in the obvious gaps, such as the introduction of other characters. I think we should:

1. Create three other main characters:
   a. The mercenary recruiter who becomes the main antagonist. From our research we find that these are the people who make the big money, the merchants of men, who lure social misfits into the service. Let's call him Frank Thorton.
   b. An official or agent of the government doing the recruiting. He is the only one who acts with compassion toward the mercenaries. Let's call him John Willoughby.
   c. A woman that Joe becomes involved with. Let's call her Mary.

2. Make the locations more precise:
   a. Joe lives in Philadelphia. From our research we know this city is one of the active recruiting areas.
   b. Joe lives in an apartment in a brownstone near one of the universities. Remember we said that he dropped out of college. The apartment is typical student fare: shabby, full of books and posters.

    c. Let's pick Rhodesia as the country in Africa where the war takes place—part of the interior where the battle zone is.

3. Add new bits of action as suggested by the basic story:
    a. When Joe and Chuck answer the ad in the magazine, they are going to have to meet the recruiters. So let's have a plush party at a fine hotel where they are sucked in by the smell of money that the recruiters use to attract prospects.
    b. To show Joe's change of heart, we can use literature, a book he finds perhaps in the pocket of a dead comrade or in one of the deserted farmhouses. Yes, he is in a big, deserted plantation house and finds a copy of a book that speaks not of war and its glorifications, but of the beauty of love and life. *Vol de Nuit* by Antoine de Saint-Exupéry, perhaps. Maybe it had been a book which he had read in college and now finally understands. He could have flashbacks to a professor reading certain passages from the book. Maybe he continues having flashbacks about other books or art. Maybe paintings that deal with the same sentiments.

Let's incorporate these last notes with the rough outline and develop a second-draft outline.

Second-draft Outline

1. Joe Bonner, a college dropout, can't find work; he lives in a university section of Philadelphia, alone and disillusioned.

2. Joe lives in a shabby apartment surrounded by his books, records, and movie posters, all glorifying war, violence, and adventure; he has many guns and other weapons of all sorts.

3. One day while at a store, Joe meets Mary, an attractive brunette, who becomes his lover.

4. One day Joe and his closest friend, Chuck, an old college buddy, answer an ad in a magazine for adventurers, calling for mercenary recruits. They receive an invitation to a reception held by the recruiters. At a posh party at a plush hotel held to sucker prospects, they are impressed by the money promised and sign a contract.

5. Frank Thorton, the American recruiter, gathers the recruits

and flies them off to Europe. Thorton takes an immediate dis-liking to Joe and Chuck.

6. In Europe, an official of the Rhodesian government, John Willoughby, shows himself to be a very sensitive person and for the first time paints a realistic picture of what the recruits might be getting themselves into. He takes a liking to Joe and Chuck and tries to warn them to go back home.

7. The mercenaries finally get to Africa and, in the capital of Rhodesia, they begin to see that things might not be as great as promised. From this point on everything seems to disintegrate. Things get worse with every mile that they travel toward the battle zone.

8. Joe and Chuck, finally faced by real violence and death, begin to realize that real war is a far cry from watching it in a movie in a comfortable theatre or reading about it in a novel.

9. They are cut off from their company and are faced with what looks like certain death. They start philosophizing about the pathology that led them to their predicament and the "not so bad after all" life back home. While waiting to die, they see the beauty in simple things.

10. After some heavy fighting, Chuck is mortally wounded and dies in Joe's arms. Joe escapes and begins working his way back to the capital. All through his flight back, Joe has flashbacks of things in his life that he did not understand the value of until now—good books that he had read, for example. Not books glorifying war, but the beauty of love and life.

11. In a deserted plantation house he finds a copy of a book he had read in college, *Vol de Nuit* by Antoine de Saint-Exupéry. He finally understands the book.

12. Joe finally works his way back to the capital and boards a ship back to the States, realizing that courage, true courage, is in fighting the peaceful battles of everyday existence.

Now we are well on our way. By adding additional material and continuing in the same manner, constantly expanding the outline and developing the plot, we will have a strong framework built of large narrative units, much like chapters in a book.

1. Introduction of main character, Joe Bonner, as a disillusioned young man, unable to find success. He lives in a university section of Philadelphia in the early 1970s.

2. Joe leaves his apartment after another futile day and, at the store, meets Mary.

3. Joe takes Mary to the movies, a film of great violence, after which they take a walk along the street and they run into Joe's friend Chuck.

4. They go to a bar and have a few drinks, where they discuss their views on life.

5. Mary takes a liking to Joe and expresses a desire to see him again. She is the first woman to take any real interest in him. Back in his apartment she is taken aback by the violent movie posters and weapons.

6. Chuck, who lives downstairs from Joe, pulls one of his many escapades and crashes into Joe's apartment with a gun. They laugh and begin joking about becoming mercenaries, hunting bandits in Bolivia.

7. One day Joe and Chuck see an ad in a magazine calling for mercenaries, and, after joking about it, Chuck answers the ad and receives an invitation to a party. After much arguing, they decide to go.

8. At the posh party, held at a plush hotel to impress the suckers, Joe and Chuck are enjoying the food, women, and general show of luxury. They are impressed by the money promised and sign a contract.

9. Joe tells Mary about the signing of the contract, and she breaks down and tries to dissuade him.

10. On a rainy night, Joe and Chuck are transported by bus to the airport with the other recruits. Frank Thorton, the American recruiter, takes an immediate dislike to the two men. While they are on a chartered flight, Joe and Chuck begin to suspect that this may not be as much fun as they thought.

11. When they are in London, Joe and Chuck are again lulled into a false sense of security by the pleasant surround-

ings. An official of the Rhodesian government, John Willoughby, shows himself to be a sensitive person and, for the first time, paints a realistic picture of what the recruits might be getting themselves into. He takes a liking to Joe and Chuck, seeing that they are different from the others, and tries to warn them, telling them to go back home.

12. The mercenaries finally get to Africa and, in the capital of Rhodesia, they begin to see that things might not be as great as promised. From this point on everything seems to disintegrate. Things get worse with every mile that they travel toward the battle zone.

13. Once in the interior of the battle zone, the reality of what they have gotten themselves into hits them like the African heat. The base camp is in shambles, ill-equipped, ill-provisioned, and ill-defended by green recruits; they are like lambs ready for the slaughter.

14. It is immediately apparent that their greatest danger is Thorton, the commander, and not the rebels. Thorton becomes ruthless in his spurring of the men into action. Without batting an eye, he shoots one recruit for refusing to fight.

15. Joe and Chuck, faced by real violence and death, begin to realize that real war is a far cry from watching it on a screen in a comfortable theatre or reading about it in a novel.

16. They are cut off after a disastrous battle and a confrontation with Thorton. Chuck is mortally wounded. They are faced with what looks like certain death. They start philosophizing about the pathology that led them to their predicament and the "not so bad after all" life back home. While waiting to die, they see the beauty in simple things.

17. Chuck dies in Joe's arms, and Joe, the only survivor, starts to work his way back to the capital and safety. During his flight he has flashbacks and memories of things in his life that he did not understand until now, such as good books that he had read, books glorifying not war, but the beauty of love and life.

18. After some narrow escapes, Joe enters a deserted plantation house for shelter from a storm. In the house he finds a lone rebel who has been hiding there. They confront each other, and Joe tries to let the rebel escape with his life.

The rebel tells Joe that he must kill him, or at least try, forcing Joe to take his life.

19. In the personal effects of the rebel, Joe finds a book, *Vol de Nuit* by Antoine de Saint-Exupéry. It is a book that he had read in college but never understood until now.

20. Joe finally works his way to the capital and, through the efforts of John Willoughby, receives the money due to him and passage on a ship to the States. On the ship Joe finds a note from Mary saying that she is waiting for him. Joe sends her a wire saying:

> As I stood at the rail watching the wild geese flying overhead on their night flight, I thought of my night flight which brought me here and will eventually take me home, and I realized that courage, true courage, is in fighting the peaceful battles of everyday existence.

chapter 3

THE TREATMENT

FROM THE CONCEPTUAL TO THE CONCRETE

At this point in the evolution of the script, we begin one of the most important phases, the *treatment*. As the name implies, the outline is used and the units within it are worked into a narrative which "treats" the words visually. The process of treating the outline filmically is accomplished in three general steps.

1. *Integration*
   a. Remove the divisions from the outline and integrate them into a narrative form.

2. *Interpretation*
   a. Replace the conceptual terms and phrases with visual imagery.
   b. Create the atmosphere and the "look" of the film. Describe locations and settings.

3. *Completion*
   a. Describe action in more depth.

b. Fill in the details of the plot.

c. Give the indications of dialogue and form the final film treatment.

In the treatment we must take words from the outline and replace them with images. A treatment can be any length—from ten pages to as long as the actual script—but, for all practical purposes, the major motion picture studios prefer no more than twenty-five pages. However, if your treatment requires it, make it as long as it takes to fully develop your outline.

The treatment is important for another reason: It might mean a sale. Some filmmakers are of the opinion that producers do not wish to wade through whole scripts but would rather read treatments. This is sometimes true if the scriptwriter is well established. However, I once posed the question to director Robert Wise, and he replied that a scriptwriter should always present a completed script.

This is especially true for beginning writers who must not only sell their scripts as films, but also must sell themselves as scriptwriters. Only having a finished script can do this. However, sometimes while pushing a script, you may be asked for the treatment instead. Play it safe and have a good treatment on file.

The outline contains the beginnings of many elements which we will develop in the treatment and fully realize later in the master scene and shooting scripts. Some of these are listed in the figure on page 18.

As we have said, we must develop these elements replacing the words with visual imagery. We take the words we mentioned from the outline and translate them into descriptive narratives in the treatment, which can then be translated into the actual images of our film as described in the script.

Let's look at an example closer to our area of interest. Let's say we have the statement "Joe and Mary meet frequently in the park." This innocent phrase is extremely difficult to illustrate. What do we do? Do we show them in the park walking toward each other over and over again? Of course not. What we must do for that simple phrase of eight

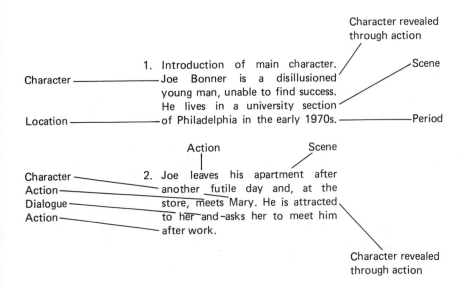

words is construct a whole series of images showing situations, circumstances, and dialogue which communicates to the viewer the fact that these two people meet in the park regularly over some distance in time.

In our outline we have the phrase "disillusioned young man, unable to find success." This is the same kind of conceptual phrase. We must now create the visual imagery which will show the meaning of the words *disillusioned* and *success.*

We want an atmosphere of desolation, so we choose the inner city which can be very lonely to someone on his own—lonely because of all the people rather than in spite of them. We show the hot asphalt of a city in summer, where the very pavement sucks at our feet to keep us down and tempers rise with the temperature. We choose dusk when the promise of the new day dies with the setting sun. Joe walks home. We show him rising out of the ground from the subway exit; his figure shimmers through the heat waves almost as though his spirit, the ghost of his dead *illusions,* rises from the underworld. He has failed another time to find work. His *illusions* are gone. We juxtapose him and the squalor of the city with all its symbols of the affluent society that he cannot afford. We show that Joe no longer believes in the American Drean.

We go through this thought process even though these words will never be read by anyone. You can see how much work and interpretation it takes to develop the treatment from the outline.

Now let's start with the first unit of the outline and see how we begin to replace words with pictures.

Introduction of main character. Joe Bonner is a disillusioned young man, unable to find success. He lives in a university section of Philadelphia in the early 1970s.	The film begins with a panoramic view of Philadelphia. It is a hot, humid summer afternoon, and the approaching evening offers no respite from the heat of the day. The heat waves rise shimmering from the hot pavement. A young man, whom we will get to know as Joe Bonner, seems to rise with the heat from the pavement as he exits the subway. He walks slowly along the street as the late afternoon sun casts long shadows.

This is what a treatment is all about, creating visual imagery. In the treatment we establish the mood, atmosphere, and look of the film. Here we describe the action in more depth, and we also give the first indications of dialogue. The actual dialogue has not been developed yet, but we begin thinking about it.

In the treatment we might have phrases like:

"Mary *explains* her reasons for not going."

"Joe *tells* her about his trip."

"She *talks* to him about not signing up."

Later in the master scene script, the dialogue must be written out completely, but for now phrases such as the above will suffice to give the information necessary for continuity and to mark the spot where the dialogue will be inserted when it is developed.

Writing a good treatment with well developed visual imagery will help you tremendously when, in the next phase of development, you must create the descriptive passages present in the screenplay's scenes and in the final shooting script's shots.

Many times I hear beginning writers and film students say that they dispense with the treatment. This is a grave error. A film is "built" in the true sense of the word: it is an elaborate construction which must be built one level at a time. The building blocks of the film or script are the *shots*. The shots, although given form only in the shooting script, are conceived in the treatment. The good scriptwriter confronts each and every phase in the script's development as if it were the most important one. As you will hear me say again, take the time and take advantage of every chance you can to improve your script. Make your mistakes on paper. Once the script is in the hands of the producer or director, it is too late.

Taking the first two units of the outline, let's look a little closer at the amplification in the treatment as shown in the following example.

With this example you can see how the first two units of the outline—five sentences of 54 words—gave us the raw material for 195 words of treatment. In the treatment we have quickly started to develop two characters and their dialogue, described several locations or settings, developed action, set the mood, and begun to develop a relationship between these two people whom we are already beginning to know.

The film begins with a panoramic view of Philadelphia. It is a hot and humid summer afternoon, and the approaching evening offers no respite from the heat of the day. A young man, whom we will get to know as Joe Bonner, seems to rise with the heat from the pavement as he exits from the subway. He walks along the street as the late afternoon sun casts long shadows.

After another futile search for work, Joe returns to his shabby apartment. In the gloom of the apartment, as he reaches into the bright pool of the refrigerator's interior for a beer, he thinks of the woman who sold him beer at a corner bar.

Joe returns to the bar. In the warm and congenial surroundings he forgets his problems and starts talking to the barmaid Mary, an attractive brunette in her late twenties. She remembers him and jokingly asks if he came back to complain about the beer he bought earlier. He tells her that he hates to drink alone and asks her if she would like to do something after she gets off from work.

After work, Joe and Mary go to a movie; it is a film of great violence, and Mary questions his choice. Joe explains that violence is a valid theme in the American cultural legacy of film and literature and that even the history of the United States is built on violence.

As they walk along the city street, absorbed in each other, they do not realize that Joe's friend Chuck King has come up alongside them; they are startled when he begins speaking. Joe introduces Chuck and Mary to each other, and they continue walking. The now cool night air puts the three in a more festive mood, and they decide to go to a bar for a few drinks.

In the bar, over drinks, the three exchange their views on life. As the night progresses, Joe and Chuck begin to carry on. They start insulting people and eventually pick a fight. Mary takes a liking to Joe in spite of his bragging and fighting and expresses a desire to see him again. Because she sees someone

OUTLINE

1. Introduction of main character. Joe Bonner is a disillusioned young man, unable to find success. He lives in a university section of Philadelphia in the early 1970s.

2. Joe leaves his apartment after another futile day and, at the store, meets Mary. He is attracted to her and asks her to meet him after work.

TREATMENT

setting ———————— The film begins with a panoramic view of Philadelphia. It is a hot, humid summer afternoon and the approaching evening offers ———— mood no respite from the heat of the day. The heat waves rise shimmering from the hot pavement.

action ——————— A young man, whom we will get to know as Joe Bonner, seems to rise with the heat from the pavement as he exits the subway. He walks ————— action

setting ——————— slowly along the street, the late afternoon sun casting long shadows. ———————————— mood

action ——————— After another futile search for work, Joe returns to his shabby apartment. In the gloom ———— mood

setting ——————— of the apartment, as he reaches into the bright pool of the refrigerator's interior for a beer, ———— action he remembers the pretty brunette who sold him

character ————— the beer at the corner bar. ———————————— setting

action ——————— Joe goes to the bar and in the warm and con- ———— mood genial surroundings he forgets his problems and

dialogue ——————— starts talking to the barmaid, Mary, an attractive brunette in her late twenties. She remem- ———— dialogue

character ————— bers him and jokingly asks if he came back to complain about the beer he bought. He tells her

development ┐ that he hates to drink alone and asks her if
& ├——— she would like to do something after she gets ——— dialogue
interaction ┘ off from work.

worth her trouble, she tries to cut through the atmospheric maze of Joe's personality. She is the first woman to take a real interest in him. She really likes him, and they leave together and go to his apartment. She is shocked by the guns, knives, and the childish symbols of masculinity.

Now that they are alone, Joe's true nature comes through; he is a relatively bright person who just can't cope with the everyday world; some of his insights into society are very perceptive, but he is socially and emotionally myopic and cannot act on those insights.

Early one morning, the sun filtering in through the apartment windows, Chuck pulls one of his many pranks, sneaking up to Joe's door and tapping on it with the barrel of a gun. Joe, getting into the spirit of the game, takes a shotgun, unlocks the door, and hides behind some furniture. When Chuck kicks open the door and bursts in, Joe jumps out and they both pretend to fire, making shooting noises. They laugh.

Over a cup of coffee they talk about hunting bandits in Bolivia or Sardinia. They become serious for a moment and talk about being born too late for adventure and being out of tune with the times. They get drunk and lie on the floor of the apartment, eating and listening to music.

The early morning finds Joe in bed. The phone rings, and he answers; Mary asks if they could do something together. They decide to meet at a coffee shop for breakfast. In the coffee shop, while a heavy rain washes the awakening city, they run into Chuck who shows Joe a magazine in which there is an ad asking for mercenaries to go to Rhodesia. Joe and Chuck joke about the ad, and Mary gets upset because she sides with the rebels. Mary thinks Joe and Chuck are being childish and morally irresponsible.

Later Chuck answers the ad. Chuck meets with Joe to tell him that he has received an answer to the ad and tells Joe that they should go to a reception being held by the mercenary recruiters. After much arguing, Joe relents and agrees to go. On a hot evening, Joe and Chuck go to the reception in a plush hotel and, in the cool air-conditioned luxury, are slowly sucked in by the glitter of the party given by the mercenary organization.

Although bright enough to see through the thin veneer of decor, fine food, and attractive women, Joe and Chuck still like what they see—enough to want to become a part of it. The recruiter Frank Thorton rubs them the wrong way and, in turn, is irritated by them. But Joe and Chuck find the money too hard to resist and sign the contract.

When Joe gets home he finds Mary waiting at his door, and they discuss his decision to go to Africa. She breaks down and tries to dissuade him with every argument available to her. She becomes bitter and, after tearing into him, walks out. Joe goes after her and tries to apologize, but she runs away.

On an unseasonably cold and rainy night, Joe and Chuck walk to the inner city and board a bus the recruiters have chartered to take them to the airport. During the ride to the airport, Joe sees his reflection in the bus window, and the city lights in the distance seen through his reflection gives him a feeling of vagueness. Somehow the transparent face on the glass seems to imply his lack of substance, that he doesn't exist anymore, that he is just a shadow of himself. As this intimation of doom washes over him, the noise of the men in the bus fades from his consciousness, replaced by an almost thundering silence as the reflection in the window screams back at him, a terrible, soundless scream.

On the chartered plane to London, Thorton begins to reveal his true character; he is a ruthless, cruel man who takes an immediate dislike to Joe and Chuck, who begin to feel that the adventure may not be as much fun as they thought.

In London, the recruits are again lulled into a false sense of security and optimism. The fine hotel and party given by the government officials again blinds Joe and Chuck to the realities, which are nonetheless beginning to appear. John Willoughby, an official of the Rhodesian government, shows himself to be a sensitive person and for the first time paints a realistic picture of the dangers the men will face. He likes Joe and Chuck and warns them to go home.

They arrive on the African continent and begin travelling toward the battle zone; although the conditions worsen, Joe is touched by the beauty of the African landscape. Stopping to rest, they see the sunset reflected on the Lampolo river which, like a pink ribbon, unwinds in a valley below them. After a short break, the convoy continues its journey on to Umtali in the south.

Finally, Joe and Chuck, who are fed up with the failure of the organization to supply adequate equipment as promised, go to their commander to complain, and he tells them that their new commander will take care of them. To their dismay, it is then that Joe and Chuck find out that their new commander is Captain Thorton, who turns up in combat fatigues.

After arriving at the run-down shambles that is their base camp, Captain Thorton and his two aides rake in great profits from the recruits by selling food and supplies. Thorton becomes ruthless in spurring the men into action before they are in any way combat-ready. One English recruit named Biff, who befriends Joe and Chuck, refuses to go into action with untrained personnel and is shot through the head by Thorton, who doesn't bat an eye.

In action, Joe and Chuck, faced now by real violence, cruelty, and death, begin to realize that adventure stripped of its romantic veneer is a far cry from watching it on a screen in a comfortable theatre. Reading about it in an easy chair is not the same as smelling the cordite and feeling the hot blood on their hands or looking into the eyes of a man they are killing or about to kill.

While out on patrol one dusty hot afternoon, the rebels attack and a great battle takes place in which most of the recruits are killed. Joe and Chuck and a few other survivors head back to camp. Along the way the other recruits desert after trying to talk Joe and Chuck into going with them. But the two return to the base to get even with Thorton and his men. Joe does not want to go back, but he does in case Chuck needs his help.

When they arrive in camp, Thorton and his men are about to leave with supplies and valuables from the dead recruits. As soon as Thorton sees the two men he starts firing at them. At the end of the shootout Chuck kills Thorton's men and is mortally wounded by Thorton. Joe kills Thorton and, with Chuck's unconscious form, flees into the bush.

The rebels overrun the whole area while Joe and Chuck start working their way back to the capital, expecting certain death.

While escaping, they begin philosophizing about the

pathology that led them to their predicament, and the "not so bad after all" life they had back home. While waiting for death, Chuck begins to comment on the beauty of simple things and the desirability of life; how strong the drive for self-preservation is in humans, and how tenaciously humans cling to life. Chuck dies in Joe's arms, leaving him alone at night on the veld to make his way back to the capital. During the escape to the capital Joe thinks of many things in his life which he never understood until now—the good works of art, the better literature glorifying not war, but love and life.

After some narrow escapes and close calls with the rebels, Joe comes upon a deserted plantation house during a violent rain storm. In the dark shambles of the interior of what once had obviously been a home of luxury, Joe comes face to face with a lone rebel who, like himself, had come to the house for shelter. Joe has the advantage, for he is armed with several automatic weapons and the rebel has only a knife.

They try to converse but they don't understand each other's language. Joe tries to let the rebel go but the rebel doesn't understand; they struggle and Joe is forced to kill him. In the personal effects of the rebel, Joe finds a book that he had read in college and only now understands. The book, *Vol de Nuit* by Antoine de Saint-Exupéry, touches Joe because, like the protagonist, danger and near death have given him an appreciation of the simple things and a love of life.

Joe finally works his way back to the capital; with the help of Willoughby, he receives his money and passage on a ship to the States. On the ship, as he is saying goodbye, Willoughby gives Joe a wire from Mary, saying that she is waiting for him and that she loves him.

And as Joe looks out at the last rays of the setting sun and the eternal sea, he thinks of the wire he has sent to Mary. Thus we hear the words of Joe's wire to Mary:

> ... and as I stood at the rail watching the wild geese flying overhead on their night flight, I thought of my night flight which had brought me here and will now take me home, and I realized that courage, true courage, is in fighting the peaceful battles of everyday existence.

chapter 4

THE SCREENPLAY

SETTING THE SCENE

The screenplay is the final form of what we commonly think of as the script. This is the form which is submitted to agents, producers, and studios. At this point, we do two important things:

1. Break the treatment down into its locations or settings.

2. Fully develop the dialogue.

The first gives us the beginnings of what will be the SCENIC HEADING in the script:

EXT.—CITY STREET—EARLY EVENING

Now that we have an understanding of the form, and we have the tools to work with, we can divide the treatment into its *locations*. We then transfer the *descriptive material* from

1. DIVIDE INTO LOCATIONS:
    The film begins with
    a panoramic view of . . .

                                            EXT.—CITY STREET—EARLY EVENING

    He walks slowly along
    the *street*, the *late*
    afternoon sun casting
    long shadows.

2. TRANSFER DESCRIPTIVE MATERIAL:

    It is a hot, humid summer   It is a hot, humid summer afternoon
    afternoon and the approach-   in Philadelphia, Pennsylvania, and
    ing evening offers no respite   the approaching evening offers no
    from the heat of the day . . .   respite from the heat of the day.
                                             JOE BONNER, a young man in his early
    . . . He walks slowly along the   thirties . . . exits the subway. He walks
    street, the late afternoon sun   slowly along the street, the late
    casting long shadows.   afternoon sun casting long shadows.

3. INSERT DIALOGUE:

                                                            JOE

                                             Mary . . . actually, I just hate
                                             to drink alone.

                                                            MARY

                                             Poor baby.

                                                            JOE

                                             No, really . . .

                                                            MARY

                                             Well, you came to the right
    He tells her that he   place.
    hates to drink alone . . .

                                             She looks around at the crush of people
                                             around them. Joe follows her gaze, and
                                             their eyes meet again.

                                                            JOE

                                             Yeah . . .

                                             They both smile.

                                                            JOE
                                                        (continuing)

                                             I guess I did.

the treatment into the numbered scenes. Finally, we insert the *dialogue* that we developed.

We go to the treatment and see what locations we have, then these locations will be the divisions of the script, what is known as master scenes, which accounts for the other name by which the script is known, the "Master Scene" script.

The screenplay or master scene script is divided by scenic headings which are numbered. The scenic headings give three bits of information:

1. Whether the scene is outside or inside, known as exterior or interior, abbreviated EXT. and INT.

2. The location: CITY STREET

3. The relative time of day: EARLY EVENING

These are then arranged in the proper order and numbered:

SCENE NUMBER • OUTSIDE OR INSIDE—LOCATION—RELATIVE TIME OF DAY

Let's look at the beginning of our treatment and see what locations are there:

Relative time of day —— The film begins with a panoramic view —— We are outside of Philadelphia. It is a hot, humid summer afternoon and the approaching evening offers no respite from the heat of the day. The young man, whom we will get to know as Joe Bonner, seems to rise with the heat from the pavement as he exits the subway. He walks slowly along the street, the late afternoon sun casting long shadows.

Location

And this gives us the information for the scenic heading:

1. EXT.—CITY STREET—EARY EVENING

The second important thing we do is develop the dialogue. From the indications of dialogue which we had in the treatment, we fully develop dialogue. From a phrase like: "She *jokes* about the beer," we develop the final dialogue under the appropriate dialogue heading:

BARMAID

That'll be two-fifty.

JOE

Two-fifty? This better be good.

BARMAID

*Well, if it's not you can always bring
it back.*

Also the action is developed further in the screenplay. We then take these elements and put them together in the proper form. This entails understanding the elements of the script. Each element has its place on the page.

In the following example we illustrate the place of each element in the shot as it appears on the script page. It is helpful to think of each element as a piece of a puzzle, which always goes in its appropriate place.

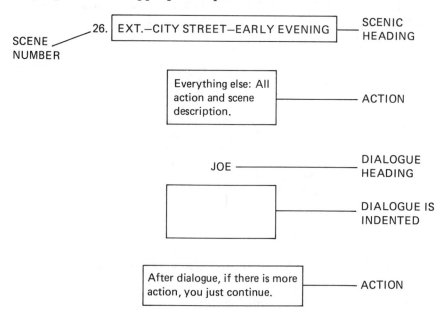

Night Flight

SAMPLE MASTER SCENE SCRIPT

1. **EXT.—CITY STREET—EARLY EVENING**   1.

   It is a hot, humid summer afternoon in Philadelphia, Pennsylvania, and the approaching evening offers no respite from the heat of the day. JOE BONNER, a young man in his early thirties, disappointed by his inability to find work and his inability to find meaning in society's answers to his questions about life, seems to rise with the heat from the pavement as he exits the subway. He walks slowly along the street, the late-afternoon sun casting long shadows. On his way home after another futile search for work, Joe passes some pubs and bars, picks up a six-pack, then enters a doorway to an old brownstone, letting himself in with a key.

2. **INT.—APARTMENT—EVENING**   2.

   Joe's apartment is shabby and dark. He walks to the refrigerator and, with a sigh, opens the door; the light

   (CONTINUED)

2. (continued)
    is bright and yellow on his face. He thinks of the warm
    yellow interior of the bar where he bought the beer
    earlier. As he reaches for a cold beer, he remembers
    the barmaid's face when she handed him the paper
    bag containing the six-pack. Joe has a flashback re-
    calling their conversation:

3. INT.—BAR—EARLY EVENING   3.
    As the BARMAID, an attractive brunette in her late twen-
    ties, hands Joe the beer:

JOE

It better be good.

BARMAID

(saucy)

*Well, if you don't like it, just bring it
back.*

4. BACK TO SCENE   4.
    Joe smiles thinking of her pretty face, shuts the re-
    frigerator door, and leaves the apartment.

5. INT.—BAR—NIGHT   5.
    Joe walks into the bar and looks around. The barmaid
    is not the same one from before. His face shows his
    disappointment as he turns and bumps into the bar-
    maid he was looking for:

BARMAID

*What's the matter, didn't you like the
beer?*

JOE

(smiles)

Yeah! But I like you better.

(CONTINUED)

5.   (continued)
She smiles back and goes about her business. In the
warm, congenial surroundings, as Joe watches the retreating form of the attractive brunette, he forgets his
problems and begins to enjoy himself. The next time
she comes close, Joe glances at her name tag:

JOE

*Mary . . . actually I just hate to drink
alone.*

MARY

Poor baby.

JOE

No, really . . .

MARY

Well, you came to the right place.

She looks at the crush of people around them. Joe follows her gaze, and as their eyes meet again:

JOE

Yeah . . .

They both smile:

JOE

(continuing)

I guess I did.

As the evening progresses, Joe sees a few friends
who say hello. Joe constantly keeps Mary in view and,
after more eye games, comments:

JOE

*Look, I really do hate being alone.
How about a drink or something?*

(CONTINUED)

5.   (continued)

MARY

*I'll be off in a little. Maybe a drink
. . . or something.*

She smiles mischievously, then she walks away as Joe
shakes his head. In a little while, Mary joins him at a
booth where he is now sitting:

JOE

*Hey . . . You're really super.
Thanks. My name's Joe.*

MARY

Joe what?

JOE

Joe Bonner.

MARY

*Look, Joe, do you mind if we just
walk a little? I have to get out of
here before I suffocate.*

JOE

No problem. Let's go.

Mary says goodbye to a few people, then they leave.

6.   EXT.—CITY STREET—NIGHT   6.
Once outside the bar a thin breeze seems to bring
comfort to them and erase any tension which might
have been present. As they walk along, making small
talk, they pass a movie theatre showing *The Wild
Bunch*:

(CONTINUED)

6.   (continued)

> ### JOE
>
> *Hey, would you like to catch a show?*

> ### MARY
>
> *What, that?*

> ### JOE
>
> *What's wrong with that? That's a classic. It deals with camaraderie and courage . . .*

> ### MARY
>
> *It deals with violence . . . and that's it. The fact that it makes a show of dealing with greater issues makes it even worse.*

> ### JOE
>
> *Look, I really like you, and let's not let it ruin our evening before it even starts. Okay?*

She smiles at him and he touches her cheek:

> ### MARY
>
> *Okay, Joe . . . okay.*

As they continue their walk, they do not notice as another young man, CHUCK KING, mid-thirties, with a beard, comes up behind them and shoves a finger into Joe's back:

> ### CHUCK
>
> *All right, man, just hand over the bread and no one will get hurt.*

Mary is uncertain about what is happening and fixes

(CONTINUED)

6. (continued)
    her eyes on Joe for a clue. Joe reaches into his jacket
    as though reaching for a gun. Joe and Chuck both
    point their fingers at each other and make shooting
    noises:

                         CHUCK
                      (continuing)
              Hi, Joe. How yah doin'?

                          JOE
              *Okay, buddy. How are you? Chuck,
              this is Mary.*

                         CHUCK
              Hi.

    Mary is a little irritated at first, but, as they walk, she
    relaxes again. Chuck shows himself to be bright, and
    the level of conversation is high. Joe and Chuck show
    themselves to be warm and sensitive. '

    The now cool night air, the cheery twinkle of neon, and
    the stimulating conversation puts them in a more fes-
    tive mood. They decide to go into a beer cellar that
    they pass.

7. INT.—BEER CELLAR—NIGHT   7.
    In the bar, over a few drinks, the three carry on a lively
    conversation which again turns to the topic of violence:

                          JOE
              *I was trying to explain that violence
              is at the base of the American
              cultural legacy of literature and film.
              Even American history itself is
              based on violence.*

                                              (CONTINUED)

7.   (continued)

> MARY
>
> *Come on, Joe. You seem too intel-*
> *ligent to believe that.*

> CHUCK
>
> *He's right . . . the trouble is that this*
> *society exists on a double stand-*
> *ard. People admire physical*
> *strength, courage, and all the clas-*
> *sic male virtues as long as it*
> *doesn't touch them. When they*
> *need help, they call a cop. But*
> *when everything is cool, cops are*
> *vulgar and callous, to be avoided.*

> JOE
>
> *Or in time of war everybody relies*
> *on the soldiers, trained to kill and*
> *destroy. They're heroes and every-*
> *body loves them and is behind*
> *them. But when the war is over, we*
> *try to forget them, they embarrass*
> *us, we try to hide them.*

> MARY
>
> *Hey! What is this? That may have*
> *been true in the past, but not today.*
> *Not after Vietnam. Today people are*
> *too aware of the realities.*

As the evening progresses, Joe and Chuck become
rowdy and start carrying on. Someone is beating his
hands on the bar as though it were a drum:

> CHUCK
>
> *Hey, that's good. Why don't you try*
> *that with your head.*

(CONTINUED)

7.   (continued)

Joe and Chuck laugh as the guy frowns at them and turns away. Mary is annoyed but can't help smiling:

> JOE
>
> *Come on, buddy, let's pop the biggest guy in here and start some action.*

Joe throws a few mock punches and bobs and weaves in his chair:

> CHUCK
>
> *Okay. I'll tap him and you back me up.*

Chuck looks around at the people and spots a big guy, with a crew cut and a battered face. Chuck motions in his direction, nodding to Joe:

> MARY
>
> *Come on! You guys are crazy. He's not bothering you. Besides, he looks like he could tear your head off.*

> JOE
>
> *Are you kidding? Chuck'll knock him into the middle of next week.*

Joe looks at Mary and smiles:

> JOE
>
> *(continuing)*
>
> *We're just kidding. Come on, where's your sense of humor?*

> MARY
>
> *You two are like little kids, you're too much.*

(CONTINUED)

7.   (continued)

Meanwhile in the next booth four men are beginning to make comments about Joe and Chuck.

One of the four men makes a funny noise:

CHUCK

(to the four men)

You said something?

1st MAN

Pardon?

CHUCK

Hey, slick. I said, did you say something?

Chuck rises to his feet:

JOE

Chuck, sit down.

CHUCK

Don't worry.

1st MAN

Yeah, I said . . . (repeats noise)

And the four start laughing uncontrollably:

JOE

The odds, Chuck. Leave them alone.

CHUCK

(mocking their laugh)

That's pretty funny, Ace. Almost as funny as your face.

(CONTINUED)

7.   (continued)

JOE

(loud)

*Chuck, the odds aren't fair. There's
only four of them. Sit down.*

By this time Mary is laughing in spite of the fact that
she is shocked by their behavior:

MARY

*Let's get out of here before some-
thing happens.* Please.

Mary begins to leave, and one of the four men makes
a lewd comment:

2nd MAN

Tasty. I'd sure like to . . .

The rest of his words are unintelligible. Mary starts
pushing Joe and Chuck toward the door. But Joe turns
and yells over his shoulder:

JOE

*It'd be too crowded, there's one
ass in there already.*

The four men react, getting out of their seats. The
three exit the bar.

8.   EXT.—CITY STREET—NIGHT   8.

Outside the bar, laughing at their own humor, they run
down the street, away from the four men. The three of
them, after eluding the four men, slow down out of
breath to rest. Still laughing, they flop down on a
stoop:

CHUCK

Hey, listen, I got to split.

(CONTINUED)

8. (continued)
                    (turning to Mary)

        *I really enjoyed meeting you. Give
        Joe a chance, Mary, he's really a
        hell of a guy.*

Chuck leaves Joe and Mary on the stoop:

                      JOE

        *Look, I hope I haven't scared you
        away. We were just having some
        fun.*

Mary stares at Joe for a while, thinking:

                     MARY

        *I like what I think I see inside of
        you, and I think I'd like to see more
        of you. Please call me again.*

She places her hand on his cheek and kisses him
softly, then quickly moves off into the night. Joe sits
quietly, lost in thought.

9. **EXT.—CITY STREET—DAY**   9.
    Joe is walking along the street with an armful of groc-
    eries and runs into Mary:

                     MARY

        Hi, Joe.

                      JOE

        Hi. You sure are tasty.

                     MARY

        Please don't start.

They laugh and start walking together:

(CONTINUED)

9.   (continued)

JOE

How have you been?

MARY

Good.

JOE

Really good to see you, Mary.

MARY

(enthusiastically)

Good to see you too, Joe.

JOE

Listen, how about coming over to my place? I just bought all these good things, and I'll cook you the best gourmet lunch you have ever had.

MARY

That sounds great, Joe. Let's go.

She takes Joe by the arm, and they go to his apartment.

10.   INT.—JOE'S APARTMENT—DAY   10.

Joe and Mary enter. Mary does a double take as she looks around the apartment. There is a great clutter of books and movie posters from westerns, police, and adventure films of every variety, all dealing with the glorification of war and violence. The walls are covered with guns and knives of every description:

(CONTINUED)

10. (continued)

> MARY
>
> *My God! You have an arsenal here.*
> *What are you expecting, a war?*

> JOE
>
> *I wish.*

> MARY
>
> *(shocked)*
>
> *What?*

> JOE
>
> *Just kidding. But I really do crave*
> *adventure. I know it's trite and over-*
> *stated, but I wish I had been born*
> *earlier.*

He assumes a British accent:

> JOE
>
> *(continuing)*
>
> *When men were men, by Jove, Bal-*
> *aclava, the thin red line, and all*
> *that.*

> MARY
>
> *You're really crazy, I swear.*

But she smiles and grabs his face in her hands. Joe grabs her and kisses her, she responds. She moves off to the kitchen area:

> MARY
>
> *(continuing)*
>
> *You're supposed to be cooking.*

(CONTINUED)

10. (continued)

Joe follows her and resumes kissing her on the face and neck:

JOE

I am, honey, I am.

She laughs and they stagger back into the stove. Joe regains his composure and begins cooking, while Mary makes drinks. Mary, drink in hand, walks around apartment looking at books:

MARY

Have you read these books, or are they here just for show?

Joe stops setting the table and stares at her:

JOE

Yes, I've read them. All of them.

MARY

You've read these books and you can still carry on like a psychotic boy scout? All that business about adventure, it's all romantic bull. Can't you see that?

JOE

It's not bull. The order of things is an order that we impose on it.

MARY

I don't understand.

Joe continues preparing the table:

JOE

You imply that the romantic view is

(CONTINUED)

10. (continued)

> *not realistic, it's idealistic or patho-*
> *logical. What I'm saying is that man*
> *imposes his own order on things,*
> *his own view or code of ethics,*
> *which he must live by. That is real-*
> *ity.*

She looks at him intently, then moves over to him and places her fingers over his lips:

MARY

> *Let's eat and then in bed you can*
> *tell me more of Man and the nature*
> *of things.*

11. INT.—STAIRWELL OF APARTMENT HOUSE—MORN-
ING 11.
The early morning sunlight streams in heavy shafts from the window on the landing. Dust particles, like smoke, float through the sunlight. Someone creeps up the stairs. As the person gets close to Joe's door, we see a gun in a hand. The hand knocks on the door with the gun barrel.

12. INT.—JOE'S APARTMENT 12.
Joe is awakened by the knock on the door. He reaches onto the night stand, picks up a handgun and, in his shorts, quietly moves to the door:

JOE

> *Who is it?*

13. INT.—HALLWAY 13.

(CONTINUED)

13. (continued)
We now see the hand cocking the hammer of the gun, with a loud click. Now we recognize the person as Chuck:

CHUCK

Chuck. I got a present for you.

14. INT.—APARTMENT   14.
Joe quietly unlocks the door and moves behind a bookcase:

JOE

It's open, come in.

Chuck kicks the door open, and both he and Joe take mock shots at each other, screaming and making shooting noises. They laugh and put the guns down:

CHUCK

Top of the morning, old bean.

(then)

Any coffee?

Joe throws on a robe, then puts water on the stove:

JOE

Come on, Chuck, let's get the hell out of here. Let's pack up and go hunt bandits in Bolivia or Sardinia. You know there are still bandits in the mountains there.

CHUCK

And Mexico too. Not too long ago a small town in Mexico was having problems with bandits. They took

(CONTINUED)

14. (continued)

> *over the whole town, and two Amer-*
> *icans went down as bounty hunters,*
> *like in the West, you know. And they*
> *had a big shootout in the middle of*
> *town. The Americans killed all the*
> *bandits . . . unbelievable.*

JOE

> *That sounds great. Come on, let's*
> *do it. Let's sell everything, get a*
> *jeep, pack up the guns, and go.*
> *Come on.*

CHUCK

> *You're kidding, I'm not. I really*
> *would do it. You weren't in Nam; I*
> *was. The bull is hard to take. You*
> *know, the discipline, power-tripping*
> *officers and so on. But when you're*
> *on your own, maybe like a merce-*
> *nary, you know, a soldier of fortune,*
> *that's different.*

JOE

> *And we're stuck here, bust a few*
> *heads in a bar, target shooting,*
> *now and then . . .*

> *(in mock seriousness)*

> *What mere mortals, bring us giants.*

Later in the same day, after much drinking, Joe and Chuck sit on the floor eating cold chicken and listen to classical music. They arm themselves to the teeth, pose in front of the fireplace, and take their pictures.

The next day, the apartment in shambles, Joe is asleep on the floor when the PHONE RINGS:

(CONTINUED)

14. (continued)

> JOE
>
> *Hello . . .*

> MARY (V.O.)
>
> *Good morning, Joe.*

> JOE
>
> *Ahhh . . . good morning, honey.
> How are you?*

15. INT.—MARY'S APARTMENT   15.

> MARY
>
> *Fine. Joe, let's do something today.
> I'd like very much to see you.*

16. JOE ON PHONE   16.

> JOE
>
> *Yeah, sure. Let's go for some cof-
> fee.*
>
> *(scratches head in pain)*
>
> *Yeah, coffee . . . downstairs at the
> coffee shop in about an hour.
> Okay?*

17. MARY ON PHONE   17.

> MARY
>
> *See you then.*
>
> *(then)*
>
> *Joe, I love you.*

18. EXT.—COFFEE SHOP—MORNING   18.
It is raining heavily, and through the window we see Jow and Mary sitting at a table, having breakfast.

19. INT.—COFFEE SHOP   19.
They are absorbed in small talk, chatting softly, almost unintelligibly, in the pleasant warm interior. In the distance, through the window, we see Chuck approaching, running to escape the rain. Chuck enters the door near their table and joins them:

CHUCK

Joe, you're gonna die . . .

Chuck pulls a magazine from his coat pocket and leafs through it:

CHUCK

(continuing)

Look at this . . .

He gives Joe the magazine, indicating something with his finger. Joe reads for a while, smiles, and looks up:

JOE

That's too much. I don't believe it.

MARY

What is it?

JOE

It's an ad for mercenaries to go to Rhodesia.

MARY

What?

(CONTINUED)

19. (continued)

CHUCK

Yeah, that's right. Excellent pay, it says . . .

Mary begins to get upset:

MARY

That's not funny, Joe. They shouldn't allow things like that to be published.

CHUCK

Well, they did.

Joe looks on, shaking his head in disbelief:

MARY

Those poor people over there are fighting for their political and economic life, against racism at its most savage.

JOE

They're just a bunch of bandits, too.

MARY

Bandits? They've been under the heel of the whites for too long, and they've had enough.

CHUCK

(gets hot)

Bull! They're communists, trouble-makers, and terrorists.

JOE

Communists? What the hell are

(CONTINUED)

19. (continued)

> communists? They're patriots fight-
> ing for their independence, come
> on. We'd do the same thing. We did
> the same thing in our revolution.

MARY

(gets up, angry)

*Look, Joe, I can't take any more of
this. I'm going up to your place.
When you're done, I'll meet you up
there.*

Mary storms out the door:

JOE

Mary, come on.

CHUCK

*Let her go. She'll calm down. I'm
just tired of bleeding hearts.*

JOE

Cool it, Chuck. Just cool it, man.

CHUCK

Hey, okay, okay.

JOE

*She's a great chick, and I don't
want to hurt her.*

CHUCK

Okay.

JOE

It's not okay.

(CONTINUED)

19. (continued)
    They sit in silence for a while:

                        CHUCK
            I sent a letter.

                         JOE
            *What letter? What the hell are you
            talking about?*

                        CHUCK
            I answered the ad.
                    (taps magazine)
            This ad.

    Joe looks at Chuck as though he were crazy:

                         JOE
            You're out of your mind, man.
                    (rises to his feet)
            I'm leaving. I'm going up.

    As Joe begins to leave:

                        CHUCK
            Just think about it, Joe.

    Joe looks back, glares at Chuck, then walks out the
    door:

                        CHUCK
                    (continuing)
            Think about it.

20. INT.—JOE'S APARTMENT—MORNING   20.
    Joe enters, soaked and wet from the rain, looks around
                                            (CONTINUED)

20. (continued)

the apartment, and sees that Mary has gone. He throws his jacket on the floor:

> JOE
>
> *(to himself)*

Damn it!

21. EXT.—CITY STREET—NIGHT   21.

Joe is walking along the street, and Chuck comes up to him:

> CHUCK
>
> *Joe. How you doing?*

> JOE
>
> *Good . . . good.*

> CHUCK
>
> *Seen Mary since the coffee shop?*

> JOE
>
> *No.*

> CHUCK
>
> *Joe, look, I'm sorry if I had anything . . .*

> JOE
>
> *That's okay, don't worry about it.*

> CHUCK
>
> *No, really I . . .*

> JOE
>
> *Don't worry about it. If that's all it*

(CONTINUED)

21. (continued)
> *takes to chase her away, she's not*
> *worth it.*

They walk in silence for a while:

CHUCK

> *I got an answer.*

JOE

> *Answer to what?*

CHUCK

> *From the mercenary recruiters.*

JOE

> *Yeah, what did they say?*

CHUCK

> *They're having a reception at a big*
> *hotel in town. It should be good. I'm*
> *going . . . You wanna go?*

Joe stops and looks at Chuck, smiles:

JOE

> *Why not. Can't dance.*

22. **EXT.—HOTEL—NIGHT**   22.
It's a hot night. Joe and Chuck walk up to the hotel
entrance, a thin veil of perspiration glistens on their
faces. They enter the lobby and sigh in relief as the air
conditioning hits them.

23. **INT.—HOTEL LOBBY**   23.

JOE

> *Oh, man, that feels good.*

(CONTINUED)

23. (continued)

CHUCK

*I'm hungry. I hope they have some-
thing good to eat.*

They enter the elevator.

24. INT.—ELEVATOR   24.

JOE

Where the hell is this thing anyway?

CHUCK

(extracts paper from pocket)

Suite 1036.

As the doors of the elevator open, Joe places his hand
on Chuck's shoulder:

JOE

I really feel stupid.

CHUCK

That's okay, you look stupid too.

They exit the elevator.

25. INT.—HOTEL SUITE   25.

The suite is plush and expensively decorated. The
room is full of people, a few uniformed men and a conspicuous overabundance of sexy women in revealing
evening clothes. In the center of the room is a long
table covered with a fine selection of canapes and
hors d'oeuvres, all clustered around a large silver tray
full of wine glasses, constantly replenished by an attendant:

(CONTINUED)

25. (continued)

> CHUCK
>
> *Man, look at that spread.*

> JOE
>
> *(looking around)*
>
> *Yeah . . . look at that spread.*

> CHUCK
>
> *I'm talking about the food, Joe.*

> JOE
>
> *Somebody went to a lot of trouble to impress us.*

> CHUCK
>
> *Yes, and they did a good job . . . I'm impressed.*

> JOE
>
> *What I mean is this is all window dressing, man.*

They help themselves to the food:

> CHUCK
>
> *I know that, but this food is real and the chicks are too.*

> JOE
>
> *Wrong, buddy boy, the chicks are unreal.*

A beautiful woman, in a most revealing outfit, approaches the two men. Her name is WENDY, a tall, sultry blonde:

(CONTINUED)

25. (continued)

> WENDY
>
> *Hi. How are you fellows tonight?*

> CHUCK
>
> *Fine.*

> WENDY
>
> *Have you met any of the members?*

> JOE
>
> *No, not yet, we just got here.*

> WENDY
>
> *Where are your name tags? I'm Wendy.*

> JOE
>
> *I'm Joe Bonner.*

> CHUCK
>
> *I'm hungry, excuse me.*

While Chuck helps himself to the food, Joe continues to talk to Wendy:

> JOE
>
> *You'll have to excuse my friend, Wendy. What he lacks in manners, he makes up in candor, which isn't a bad trade.*

Wendy leads Joe over to a table where two men are talking, one in uniform and the other in an expensive dark suit, FRANK THORTON, the mercenary recruiter, who is tall and muscular, with a rugged, darkly tanned face:

(CONTINUED)

25. (continued)

WENDY

*Major Rhodes ... Frank Thorton
... this is Joe Bonner.*

MAJOR

How do you do.

THORTON

Hi, Joe ...

Thorton extends his large hand and almost crushes the smaller man's fingers in the handshake. Thorton's thin, cruel smile just barely hides a less agreeable disposition given away by the glint of his cold blue eyes:

THORTON

(continuing)

*Excuse me, Joe, I have to break for
five.*

Joe flexes his fingers:

JOE

You already did.

Joe smiles at Thorton who turns sharply and moves away with Wendy, but not before clenching his jaw muscles and shooting Joe a sidelong glance that opens for a moment that special window behind everyone's eyes. Joe turns to Chuck who comes up with two drinks:

JOE

(continuing)

*That bastard about broke my hand.
No sense of humor either.*

As the evening progresses, Joe and Chuck become

(CONTINUED)

25. (continued)

more and more drunk and, while still in control of themselves, begin to be sucked in by the power politics of the recruiters. They show films of the latest equipment being used by the mercenaries in Rhodesia, and others showing the beautifully new, well-equipped facilities of the Rhodesian camps and bases:

MAJOR

Of course, this will mean nothing to most of you until you get to the front. What will interest you is the pecuniary remuneration.

There are some puzzled looks and "Huhs" and "Whats" from the men:

MAJOR

(continuing)

Money my lads, money!

There is a mixture of laughter and applause:

MAJOR

(continuing)

For the signing of our "one tour of duty" contract, each recruit will receive nineteen thousand five hundred Rhodesian dollars, or approximately thirty thousand U.S. dollars, for one six-month tour of duty.

The men whistle and applaud:

MAJOR

(continuing)

Thank you. Mr. Thorton and I are willing to answer any questions.

(CONTINUED)

25. (continued)

Joe and Chuck look at each other, thinking:

> CHUCK
>
> *That's not bad, old bean. Thirty thousand for six months.*

> JOE
>
> *No, but it's no picnic, for Christ's sake.*
>
> *(takes sip of drink)*
>
> *It's still a war, damn it . . .*
>
> *(almost to himself)*
>
> *The revolutionaries always win those damn wars anyway.*

> CHUCK
>
> *What the hell are you mumbling about? Come on, let's go.*

> JOE
>
> *Go where?*

> CHUCK
>
> *Sign the contracts. Come on. You still can change your mind, up until the time you leave London. You heard him. Come on, let's go.*

> JOE
>
> *(as they rise to their feet)*
>
> *I still don't like it . . .*

> CHUCK
>
> *You want to be a writer, this will*

(CONTINUED)

25. (continued)
> *give you something to write ...*
> *right? Right. Come on, you lazy*
> *bastard.*

JOE

> *I'm coming, damn it, I'm coming.*

26. INT.—JOE'S APARTMENT—NIGHT   26.
Joe lets himself in amid great noise and grumbling:

JOE

> *The Federales always lose ...*
> *those ...*

MARY (o.s.)

> *What are you mumbling about?*

Joe spins around and sees Mary lying in bed, sleepily rubbing her eyes:

JOE

> *Mary! I thought I'd never see you*
> *again.*

Joe is really feeling the booze at this point:

JOE

(continuing)

> *I'm glad you came back ...*

He fumbles with her on the bed:

JOE

(continuing)

> *I love you.*

(CONTINUED)

26. (continued)

And then he kisses her and falls onto the bed. The next morning Joe awakes to the sound and smell of eggs and bacon cooking in the kitchen. Mary is in the kitchen doing the cooking, in only a pajama top. Joe rubs his head and lights a cigarette. He moves over to her and gives her a kiss. He looks disturbed:

> MARY
>
> *Joe, I'm going to move in here and take care of you. I'm sorry I got upset. I wasn't fair to you.*

Joe begins to mill about, nervously:

> JOE
>
> *Mary, I . . .*

> MARY
>
> *You don't have to say anything. I know what . . .*

> JOE
>
> *(angry)*
>
> *You don't know anything. You don't know anything.*

> MARY
>
> *What's wrong?*

> JOE
>
> *I signed up.*

> MARY
>
> *Signed what? What are you talking about?*

(CONTINUED)

26. (continued)

                    JOE

> *I'm talking about you and me. I
> signed a contract to go to Rho-
> desia.*

She stares at him in disbelief:

                    MARY

> *What? You what?*

She rushes to him and starts slapping him across his
face:

                    MARY

                (continuing)

> *You what? You stupid jerk.*

Joe tries to settle her down:

                    JOE

> *Calm down. It's not the end of the
> world, for Christ's sake.*

She stops fighting him and stares at him, coldly:

                    MARY

> *You really don't see, do you? You
> really don't see what you're doing,
> do you?*

                    JOE

> *I'll be back in six months. If you
> really care, it'll hold.*

Again, Joe mills around the apartment, nervously:

                    JOE

                (continuing)

> *I've got to do something. Don't you*

(CONTINUED)

26. (continued)

> understand? I've had nothing but
> bad luck, I've got to turn it around.
> I'm underqualified for the good jobs
> and overqualified for the bad ones.

MARY

Joe, I . . .

JOE

*You want to hear something funny,
huh? Do you?*

MARY

Joe, please . . .

JOE

*I was turned down at a hot dog
stand. Do you hear me?*

> *(begins crying)*

*I stood there and the guy told me
that I couldn't handle selling hot
dogs.*

> *(slams fist on table)*

*He told me that I was not the type
that they needed . . . not dynamic
enough . . .*

> *(punches wall)*

sell hot dogs.

Joe breaks down. Mary runs to him and holds him in
her arms:

MARY

You'll make it, Joe. You will, and if

(CONTINUED)

26. (continued)

> you don't, it doesn't matter. You just
> keep trying. The important thing is
> that you keep trying. That is what
> life is all about, Joe. That is the
> meaning behind it all. That is the
> secret that women know.

JOE

> I know, but it's hard to settle for
> less than the top. Everyday, wher-
> ever you go, you are surrounded by
> plenty . . . you know, every maga-
> zine, commercial, shows beautiful
> people, in beautiful places, sur-
> rounded by expensive things, en-
> joying themselves. We're condi-
> tioned to want those things, damn
> it. But they don't supply us with any
> means to obtain them.

MARY

> Honey, please . . .

JOE

> No, let me finish. Today, without
> money, you're nothing . . . and it's a
> fact of life. You know everybody
> can't be millionaires, but they make
> everybody want it . . . that's the
> crime. I want it and I'm going to get
> it and nothing is going to stop me
> . . . nothing.

27. EXT.—VETS CLUB—NIGHT   27.

On an unseasonably cold night, Joe and Chuck walk
along the street, carrying duffle bags. They stop in

(CONTINUED)

27. (continued)
    front of the club, which is located in a rundown section
    of the city. A drizzle begins to fall. While they talk,
    other men begin filtering into the club:

                    JOE

        Well, I hope we didn't make a mis-
        take.

                    CHUCK

        What mistake? We haven't even
        started yet. There will be plenty of
        time for mistakes once we get there.

                    JOE

        I don't know. It's just a feeling, I
        guess.

    An old man comes out of the club and motions to the
    men as a bus pulls up:

                    OLD MAN

        Okay, let's go, come on, everybody,
        in the bus.

                    JOE

        I'm coming.

                    OLD MAN

        Yeah, so's Christmas.

    Everybody starts boarding the bus.

28. **INT. BUS**   28.
    which is now moving out of the city. Joe and Chuck
    are seated in the front row:

                                                    (CONTINUED)

28. (continued)

> JOE
>
> *When do we get to the airport?*

> CHUCK
>
> *I'm not sure. But we're suppose' to take off at one-thirty this morning.*

Joe lights a cigarette and stares out the window at the skyline. His reflection in the window and the city lights in the distance seen through his reflection gives him a feeling of vagueness. Somehow his transparent face on the rain-covered glass bothers him; it seems to imply a lack of substance, that he doesn't exist anymore, that he is just a shadow.

As this intimation of doom washes over him, the noise of the men in the bus fades from his consciousness, replaced by an almost thundering silence which becomes the roar of airplane engines. The reflection in the window screams back at him, a terrible, soundless scream.

29. INT.—PLANE—NIGHT   29.

On the flight over the Atlantic to London, Thorton begins to reveal his true character. He is ruthless and cruel, and he takes an immediate dislike to Joe and Chuck:

> JOE
>
> *If this is an example of the kind of equipment supplied by this bunch, we are in big trouble.*

> CHUCK
>
> *It's not that bad. What the hell did you expect?*

(CONTINUED)

29. (continued)

> JOE
>
> *I don't know, myself.*
>
> *(sees Thorton coming)*
>
> *Frank? Is there anything to drink in here? I'm . . .*

> THORTON
>
> *What the hell do you think this is, Bonner? This ain't no friggin' cham-pagne flight.*

The other men start laughing as Thorton starts to walk away. Joe looks at Chuck and indicates with his eyes a duffel bag behind Thorton's feet:

> JOE
>
> *Hey! Sorry I asked.*

Chuck pushes the bag farther out into the aisle; Thorton trips over it, falling flat on his face. The men roar in laughter. Thorton picks himself up and rushes to Joe and Chuck:

> THORTON
>
> *You . . .*

Thorton grabs Joe by his shirt front and pulls him out of the seat. Joe breaks his hold and punches him in the face. Thorton grins and starts to come back at Joe when the copilot appears and calls him into the cock-pit:

> COPILOT
>
> *Thorton! I won't have brawling on my plane. Do you understand?*
>
> *(then)*
>
> *Willoughby's on the wire.*

(CONTINUED)

29. (continued)
The copilot goes back into the cockpit and Thorton follows, stopping at the door:

> THORTON
>
> *Later, Bonner . . . later.*

30. INT.—HOTEL ROOM IN LONDON—EARLY EVENING 30.
The last rays of the sun stream into the otherwise dim
interior of the room, illuminating the sleeping forms of
Joe and Chuck. The PHONE RINGS, and Chuck slowly
reaches for it in his sleep:

> CHUCK
>
> *Hello . . . Yeah? Okay . . . in half an
> hour? Okay. Yeah . . . yeah . . . all
> right.*

> JOE
>
> *(sleepily)*
>
> *What's up?*

> CHUCK
>
> *We have a meeting with this
> Willoughby guy in half an hour.*

31. INT.—MEETING ROOM—NIGHT   31.
It is a large room in the hotel with chairs and a
podium, full of mercenary recruits. JOHN WILLOUGH-
BY, an official of the Rhodesian government, distin-
guished-looking, is addressing the men:

> WILLOUGHBY
>
> *. . . and the important thing is that
> my government thinks it imperative*

(CONTINUED)

31. (continued)

> *that you men understand the situation. I don't know what you have been told, but you will be facing a determined enemy. Not a bunch of barefoot savages, but a good fighting force with many victories under its collective belt . . .*

The men start to become serious:

WILLOUGHBY

(continuing)

> *The rebels consider themselves patriots, and therefore have right on their side, to their way of thinking. They are fighting for their homeland, and you are not, which gives them another edge. They operate from passion and conviction . . . and you from a cold, rational, professional point. Historically, mercenaries have not been militarily effective . . .*

The men become a bit nervous:

WILLOUGHBY

(continuing)

> *You will be effective primarily from a psychological point of view, and you will be relieving regular troops for service in more important areas. This is your last chance to back out, and I would advise those of you with any doubts to do so.*

> *(then)*

> *Thank you and good luck.*

(CONTINUED)

31. (continued)

> JOE
>
> *What do you think, Chuck?*

> CHUCK
>
> *What do you mean, what do I think? Do you have the money to pay them back for the round trip?*

> JOE
>
> *Yeah, I suppose. Besides, at least Thorton isn't around anymore.*

Willoughby walks by and Joe stops him:

> JOE
>
> *(continuing)*
>
> *Mr. Willoughby? Is the picture you painted as bad as it seems?*

> WILLOUGHBY
>
> *(looking at name tag)*
>
> *Mr. Bonner, the picture I painted is an optimistic one.*

> JOE
>
> *Optimistic? We were told that the enemy was an undisciplined, unorganized rebel.*

> WILLOUGHBY
>
> *Not hardly ... Why are you here, Mr. Bonner?*

> JOE
>
> *I need ... ah ... the money, and I want the action.*

(CONTINUED)

31. (continued)

> WILLOUGHBY
>
> *Well, my dear Mr. Bonner, that is precisely what you will get.*

He starts to leave and then stops, turns back to Joe:

> WILLOUGHBY
>
> *(continuing)*
>
> *Bonner, you seem to be an intelligent chap, not like many we get here ... you know, transients, broken men, psychopaths. Go home, Mr. Bonner, before you get more than you bargained for.*
>
> *(then)*
>
> *Excuse me.*

Chuck moves close to Joe:

> CHUCK
>
> *What did he have to say?*

> JOE
>
> *(sarcastic)*
>
> *He told me that I wasn't like the rest of the human flotsam that takes jobs like this. ... He told me to ... go home.*

> CHUCK
>
> *Maybe he's right.*

> JOE
>
> *It's too late now ... Besides, it can't be that bad.*

32. EXT.—RHODESIAN VELD—DAY   32.

The sun beats down on a convoy of a few trucks and jeeps travelling along a highway from Salisbury to Umtali in the south. The men are cheerful, talking and joking as they travel:

> CHUCK
>
> *Joe, when did they say we would be in Umtali?*

> JOE
>
> *Sometime tomorrow evening.*

Joe lights a cigarette, looks out over the countryside in obvious pleasure:

> JOE
>
> *(continuing)*
>
> *Look at that ... This country is beautiful. I can see why these people want to hold on to it. I love these grasslands.*

> CHUCK
>
> *When do we get our supplies? They tell us about the fantastic equipment, and we leave Salisbury with the clothes on our back.*

> JOE
>
> *Stop bitching ... that's all you do. What the hell's wrong with you?*

> CHUCK
>
> *I just don't like it ...*
>
> *(pulls Joe close)*
>
> *This is serious business, damn it.*

(CONTINUED)

32. (continued)

> JOE
>
> *What is?*

> CHUCK
>
> *Look at this truck.*

> JOE
>
> *What about it?*

> CHUCK
>
> *Is this the equipment described to us? Is this an armored personnel carrier?*

> JOE
>
> *Okay. But it's a good truck.*

> CHUCK
>
> *That's not the point. This is not what it's suppose' to be ... and that's not professional. I just hope it's not symptomatic of the whole damn operation down here.*

Now Joe looks worried:

> JOE
>
> *I see what you mean ...*
>
> (to himself)
>
> *If things are less than promised here, close to the capital ... what the hell will we find ... ?*

Chuck nods his head in agreement:

> CHUCK
>
> *Yeah ... in Zulu land.*

33. EXT.—BASE—DAY   33.
    The convoy arrives at the base where they stop for the
    night. This base is even worse than they expected.
    The buildings are dilapidated, the grounds are run-
    down, and the vehicles in which they are to continue
    on the last leg of the trip to the battle zone are beat-up
    junks. Joe and Chuck are disturbed by the sight of it
    all:

                        CHUCK
          My God! Look at that.

                         JOE
          What the hell is this? And you were
          complaining about the other trucks.

                        CHUCK
          Come on.

    They reach the commander's headquarters and are
    admitted to see him.

34. INT—HEADQUARTERS   34.
    THE COMMANDER, a Rhodesian army officer, is sitting
    behind his desk with a pile of papers in front of him:

                      COMMANDER
          Yes, what is it?

                        CHUCK
          Sir, we are a little concerned about
          the conditions here and the vehicles
          . . .

                      COMMANDER
          What about them?

                                              (CONTINUED)

34. (continued)

> JOE
>
> *They don't exactly inspire confidence in the operation.*

> CHUCK
>
> *They're falling apart . . . I think . . .*

> COMMANDER
>
> *(now annoyed)*
>
> *That's what we have to work with. I'm sorry.*

> JOE
>
> *Sir, what we have here is a far cry from the travelogue we were shown in the States. Everyone is complaining, sir. . . . We're just the only ones who have the guts to say anything.*

The commander now stands up:

> COMMANDER
>
> *We are far from Salisbury and, as such, must make do with what we have . . . and as far as the men are concerned, the new commander will have to deal with that . . .*

The door opens behind them:

> COMMANDER
>
> *(continuing)*
>
> *Ah . . . here he is now.*

Joe and Chuck turn and look into the cold blue eyes of Captain Frank Thorton, now wearing combat fatigues, a .45 automatic strapped to his hip.

(CONTINUED)

34. (continued)

COMMANDER

(continuing)

Captain Thorton ... you will take care of these men and their complaints, won't you?

Thorton grins:

THORTON

Certainly, commander ... I will take care of these men and the other recruits personally ... as soon as we reach Umtali ... later.

COMMANDER

That will be all.

Joe and Chuck exit, exchanging glances.

35. EXT.—HEADQUARTERS   35.

Joe and Chuck step out of the makeshift command building:

JOE

Well, that does it. We're in good hands now.

CHUCK

Yeah ... only they're around our necks.

36. EXT.—DIRT ROAD—LATE AFTERNOON   36.

The small convoy of rickety vehicles are strung out on the dirt road, clouds of dust trailing out behind them. The men in the last truck, where Joe and Chuck are

(CONTINUED)

36. (continued)
    riding, have handkerchiefs tied over their mouths and noses. Their dust-caked faces turned toward each other:

> JOE
>
> *I bet we can thank our friend for being stuck at the tail end of this parade.*

> CHUCK
>
> *Hey, you're pretty bright.*

As they reach the crest of a hill, a light wind blows away the dust and they can see the sunset reflected on the Lampolo river, which, like a pink ribbon, bends in the valley below:

> JOE
>
> *Look at that!*

> CHUCK
>
> *Yes it is . . . yes it is.*

> JOE
>
> *It must have looked just like this to the first Portuguese who came here . . . I wonder if they came like we did?*

> CHUCK
>
> *By plane . . . ? No, I don't think so.*

> JOE
>
> *No seriously, I mean, I wonder if they came for the same reasons.*

(CONTINUED)

36. (continued)

> CHUCK
>
> *I don't think so . . .*

They are interrupted by Thorton who drives up in a jeep, to where they are breaking:

> THORTON
>
> *Come on, you scum, this ain't no picnic . . .*

> JOE
>
> *Just enjoying the fresh air, Captain.*

> THORTON
>
> *You better . . . soon you'll be smell-ing Bantu armpits.*

Thorton laughs and goes back to his jeep. As they descend into the valley, the base camp—their final destination—comes into view. Finally, the reality of what they have gotten themselves into hits them like the heat of the African sun. The men are shocked by what they see.

37. **INT. BARRACKS—LATE AFTERNOON**   37.

The hot sun streams through the broken walls and shattered windows of the barracks. In the long, dusty shafts of sunlight, stirred here and there by flies and other insects, can be seen rusty cots. Here and there, other recruits, like ghosts in the shadows, stare in fear at the newcomers:

> JOE
>
> *What the hell's this? What's wrong here?*

(CONTINUED)

37. (continued)

CHUCK

What's wrong . . . ?

(angry)

*Do you have eyes, damn, it? Look.
This place is falling apart. The only
men we find here are other recruits,
look at their eyes. What are they so
scared of?*

Joe and Chuck walk outside.

38. EXT.—CAMP   38.

JOE

*Well, I have a strange feeling it
won't take us long to find out.*

At those words a couple of shells explode in the clearing in the center of the camp, and then there is silence. Thorton runs by:

CHUCK

Thorton!

He grabs the Captain's arm:

THORTON

Captain, soldier . . . it's Captain.

With the Captain are two aides, CARTER and RICHARD-
SON, whom he brought with him from the last camp.
Carter sucker-punches Chuck. As Chuck starts to
come back at Thorton, his two aides reach for their
side arms, and Joe holds Chuck back, while he pulls
his own pistol and pretends to side with Thorton, holding his .45 automatic in the general direction of the
three:

(CONTINUED)

ntinued)

be supplied with all the necessary equipment.

CARTER

And . . . ?

1st RECRUIT

And we now find out that if we want any of that fancy stuff that sold us in the first place, we'll have to pay for it.

2nd RECRUIT

That's bull and we won't stand for it.

RICHARDSON

You will be issued the standard military gear . . . but if you wish anything extra . . .

1st RECRUIT

The point is that we were promised that equipment . . . if not, we wouldn't have come, damn it.

2nd RECRUIT

Where are the fancy installations we were promised? This is a hole. . . . Where's the hospital?

CARTER

Look, soldier, I told you what the story is. Now, if you have any further complaints, let's go into the Captain's office. We don't want to

(CONTINUED)

38. (continued)

JOE

Hey! Calm down . . . take it easy, man. The Captain's right, he's doing his job. He's all right, Captain sir. Just a little scared from the shells, that's all.

Carter and Richardson again move toward Joe and Chuck. Joe fires a few rounds into the air above their heads:

JOE

(continuing)

See? Shooting makes everyone a bit jumpy, right?

A few of the men start to laugh, and the crisis is past. The two aides stop and lower their guns, looking at the Captain questioningly:

THORTON

Okay . . . calm down, boys.

(turns to Chuck)

You just remember it's Captain, and don't ever grab me again, soldier, or I'll put a bullet in your head.

Thorton and his aides walk away:

CHUCK

(to himself)

Yeah . . . I bet you would.

An English recruit, BIFF, who was in the camp when they arrived, comes over to Joe and Chuck:

BIFF

You two blokes like a whiskey?

(CONTINUED)

38. (continued)

CHUCK

No.

JOE

Yes we would . . . thanks, buddy.

(to Chuck)

Come on, we need a drink.

39. INT.—BARRACKS—NIGHT   39.

Once inside the barracks Biff pulls a bottle out of his gear and pours the two a drink, then takes a swig out of the bottle. The few men who are in the barracks leave in a hurry:

CHUCK

What's their problem?

BIFF

You're poison, mates.

JOE

Because of what happened out there?

BIFF

That's right. You've just signed your death warrants, and they want no part of you lest they be included.

JOE

What about you?

BIFF

I hate the bloody bastard, and I'm

(CONTINUED)

38. (continued)

on the blacklist, too . . .
are three of us. . . .

Biff takes another swig and refills

BIFF

(continuing)

and them's better odds.

They smile and drink up.

40. INT.—HEADQUARTERS—MORNIN

The interior, while not luxurious, is
able than the barracks. In the same
ply store of sorts, the counter of wh
Captain's office. Thorton sits at his
cruits file in to the supply counter. /
enter the room, a couple of recruits
the Captain:

1st RECRUIT

. . . but we were told that
stuff would be supplied by
ganization.

THORTON

My aides will take care of an
plaints you may have . . .

(to his aides)

Carter. Richardson. Please
care of these men.

Thorton returns to his office:

2nd RECRUIT

Look, we were told that we

39. (c

40. (continued)

> *hold up the whole operation, do we?*

Carter indicates the door to Thorton's office, and the four men disappear inside. They look back at the other men as though a doubt had entered their minds. As the door is closing over the scene, Thorton's eyes stare across the two rooms and bore into Joe's, almost saying "This is for you, Bonner, for you and your friend. Remember, *later*?" Joe's expression tells us that he has received Thorton's message.

41. INT.—MESS HALL—LATE MORNING   41.

Some men are having coffee. The two recruits, who had complained earlier, come into the mess. They walk slowly with their heads bowed. As they get closer, the men become silent, noticing that they have been savagely beaten. Joe, Chuck, and Biff, who are also having coffee with the other men, run over when they see them:

                         BIFF

> *That bastard and his two goons. . . .*
> *Look what they've done to these chaps. . . .*

Biff helps them sit down:

                         BIFF

                      (continuing)

> *. . . that's a bloody shame, that's what it is, a bloody shame.*

                         CHUCK

> *I was a paramedic, let me look at them . . .*

                                      (CONTINUED)

40. (continued)

> *(examines their faces)*
>
> *Contrary to what is usually done, these men were only beaten where it shows.*

JOE

> *You mean they were to be some kind of example for the rest of us?*

BIFF

> *That's exactly what he means, lad. After they sell all the supplies, equipment, and food that they can, then they'll not care what happens to us. Then Thorton will sooner kill you than spit.*

CHUCK

> *They're pretty bad, they might even have concussions . . . That guy's a hard case.*

JOE

> *He's a bad one, all right. I wonder what he's like in action.*

Chuck puts some gauze bandages on the men's faces from his personal supplies:

CHUCK

> *Well, I think we will soon find out. After that shelling yesterday, it won't be long before we engage.*

Biff pulls his bottle from his pack:

BIFF

> *We better not. We were supposed*

(CONTINUED)

41. (continued)

> *to receive training from these blokes with all that special equipment, and until we do I'm not going out there.*

42. EXT.—CAMP—AFTERNOON 42.

As the camp is quiet and calm, the recruits are a bit lax and everyone is taken unawares when the camp is attacked by rebels. First, several shells explode and various rockets slam into the camp, then the rebels attack. Joe and Chuck are in the barracks when the attack comes and they are better prepared. But in the center clearing of the camp and on the periphery of the compound there is havoc. Just as quickly as it begins the attack ends. In the confusion, Joe, Chuck, and Biff walk among the smoke and wreckage:

JOE

Look at the mess . . . Jesus.

CHUCK

Thank God there weren't too many of them.

BIFF

They were just teasing, lad . . . a small scouting group . . . the same one that fired those two rounds yesterday. That's why we couldn't find them, it's such a small group they move too quickly.

CHUCK

You're not new at this, Biff, but you're a recruit.

(CONTINUED)

42. (continued)

> BIFF
>
> *Aye, lad, I'm not new at this. I cut my teeth in the Congo. The fighting was worse, but the organization was better.*

They return to the barracks. As they walk:

> JOE
>
> *Why are you here? White Power?*

> BIFF
>
> *Kill the Zulu? No. I've nothing against these people. They are patriots . . . Africans.*

It is now early evening and the last rays of the sun have just disappeared, and the fires and lamps have been lighted:

> BIFF
>
> *(continuing)*
>
> *The ancient name of this country is Zimbabwe, after the ancient city and civilization by the same name. No one knows who built it, but some say that this Zimbabwe was the ancient kingdom of Ophir or King Solomon's mines. It was built before 1100 A.D. The Portuguese were the first Europeans to come here in the 16th century. The Portuguese fought the Nguni, then the Zulu fought with the British, and White Power, backed by British firearms, won over the warrior tradition and spears of the Zulu.*

(CONTINUED)

42. (continued)

> *(then)*
>
> *That's why I'm here.*

43. **EXT.—CAMP—MORNING** 43.

All the men are gathered in the clearing in the middle of camp. They are in formation, waiting for the captain. Thorton walks out and, with Carter and Richardson standing behind him, addresses the men:

> **THORTON**
>
> *Yesterday, the rebels attacked this camp. Today, we are going to seek them out and destroy them.*

The men seem to be a bit distraught and begin to murmur:

> **THORTON**
>
> *(continuing)*
>
> *We will be leaving in one hour. So get ready and be in this clearing in sixty minutes. Get light combat gear, we have to move fast. Now move.*

All the men clear out except for Biff and a few others:

> **CARTER**
>
> *Get moving, you scum.*

But no one moves. Richardson moves up to the men:

> **RICHARDSON**
>
> *If you don't move, you'll be shot for refusal to obey orders.*

The others glance at Biff and move out, leaving him standing alone. Thorton pulls his pistol and steps up to Biff:

(CONTINUED)

43. (continued)

> THORTON
>
> *Soldier, I'm only going to say it once
> . . . move out.*

> BIFF
>
> *No, sir. This force is ill-equipped
> and unprepared. They have not re-
> ceived the equipment promised, nor
> have they received any training, and
> I'll be damned if I'm going to have
> them at my back. And you're a
> bloody fool if* you go.

Thorton quickly raises his hand and points the gun at
Biff's head. Joe stretches his hand out and starts to
run to Biff, but Chuck holds him back:

> JOE
>
> *No!*

The shot rips through Biff's head before he has a
chance to defend himself:

> JOE
>
> *(continuing)*
>
> *You bastard. You bloody . . .*

Before he has a chance to say more, Chuck drags him
back to the barracks.

44. INT.—BARRACKS   44.

> JOE
>
> *(continuing)*
>
> *That son of a bitch shot him in the
> head without batting an eye. I
> watched him . . . it didn't faze him.*

(CONTINUED)

44. (continued)
Joe slams his fist into the wall while tears run down his
face:

JOE

(continuing)

I'm going to kill that bastard.

CHUCK

*And I'll help you, but you have to
wait, bide your time until it's right,
and then we'll squash him like a
bug.*

Chuck slams his boot down onto the floor.

45. EXT.—VELD—DAY   45.
Heavy boots and horses hooves crush the dry grass
as the mercenaries trek single file. The commander
Thorton and his aides Carter and Richardson ride the
horses while the recruits are on foot:

JOE

*Why are they riding and we are
walking?*

CHUCK

*They use them for hunting cattle
rustlers when they're not in the regular army.*

JOE

*It's the Wyatt Earp syndrome,
Chuck. They're playing cowboys,
and you gotta have a horse.*

Chuck gestures toward the man in front of him:

(CONTINUED)

45. (continued)

> CHUCK
>
> *Like this clown in front of us. I won-*
> *der how much he paid Thorton for*
> *that special gear.*

Then the first of a series of three shots slam into the man's body, spinning him around and causing him to fall open-armed on Joe. Now in action, Joe realizes that real violence, cruelty, and death, stripped of their romantic veneers, are a far cry from what we see on the screen or what we read in books.

In the confusion of battle, most of the recruits are killed immediately, but Joe and Chuck and a handful of others manage to make it out alive. As they retreat, they lose sight of Thorton, Carter, and Richardson:

> JOE
>
> *Where the hell is Thorton?*

> CHUCK
>
> *He's covering his ass . . . He cut out*
> *before we started shooting our way*
> *out.*

> JOE
>
> *They're all dead, Chuck. This is in-*
> *sane. We didn't know what was*
> *going on. Crazy. All this way and*
> *we get wiped out after the first en-*
> *gagement.*

> 1st RECRUIT
>
> *What are you going to do now?*

> CHUCK
>
> *Back to camp.*

(CONTINUED)

45. (continued)

> 2nd RECRUIT
>
> *Not me, pal, I'm going back to Salis-*
> *bury and back home.*

> JOE
>
> *That sounds good to me. What do*
> *you say, Chuck?*

> CHUCK
>
> *I said, I'm going back to camp. . . .*
> *I'm going to kill him.*

> JOE
>
> *For Christ's sake, Chuck, let it alone.*
> *We have the chance to go now.*

> 1st RECRUIT
>
> *We're leaving . . .*
>
> (to Joe)
>
> *Are you coming with us?*

Joe looks questioningly at Chuck who, tired of waiting, throws his pipe on the ground:

> CHUCK
>
> *I'm going to kill that animal.*

Chuck throws his compass down on the ground, at the feet of the men:

> CHUCK
>
> (continuing)
>
> *Here, go back with them.*

> JOE
>
> *Ahhh . . . hell, I'm coming . . .*

(CONTINUED)

45. (continued)
Joe turns to the others and shakes hands with them:

JOE
(continuing)
Good luck.

1st RECRUIT
Good luck to you, mate.

46. EXT.—VELD—NIGHT   46.
The landscape, the tall grass and bushes, moving
gently in the soft wind, are illuminated by the pale blue
light of the moon. Joe and Chuck reach the outskirts of
the camp undetected and, from their hiding place, see
the camp clearing.

47. EXT.—CAMP
Thorton and his men are finishing loading a jeep with
supplies and valuables from the dead recruits:

JOE
What now?

CHUCK
I'm going to kill him.

Joe tries to stop him, but Chuck begins moving out
into the open:

JOE
*Chuck, what's the use, what's the
sense of it? Chuck . . .*

Chuck is now running into the clearing, firing his automatic rifle. Thorton and his aides at the jeep are taken

(CONTINUED)

47. (continued)
by surprise. Carter and Richardson are shot down immediately. Thorton, however, being on the other side of the jeep, is protected from Chuck's barrage of bullets and manages to get off a burst from his machine gun, which severely wounds Chuck. Meanwhile, Joe runs firing from the cover of the trees, forcing Thorton to take cover behind the jeep, but not before dropping his machine gun:

JOE

Thorton . . . you son of a bitch . . .

Joe keeps shooting as he runs toward Thorton. As he rounds the jeep, Thorton closes with him taking the inexperienced man by surprise. The force of Thorton's attack knocks the rifle out of Joe's hands. Thorton has a bayonet in his hand, and Joe manages to pull his own bayonet during the struggle. The two men fight until Joe finally kills Thorton. Then Joe drags his unconscious friend into the bush. The rebels overrun the whole area. Joe and Chuck start working their way back to the capital.

48. EXT.—VELD—NIGHT   48.
In the background we HEAR the rebels DESTROYING the camp as Joe struggles with Chuck to put as much distance as possible between them and the rebels:

CHUCK

What did you do with Thorton?

JOE

I killed him.

CHUCK

Good . . . good . . . I'm dying, Joe.

(CONTINUED)

48. (continued)

                    JOE

*You wanted it, damn it. Why didn't
you come away with us? Why didn't
we leave with the others? Damn it.
Why did you have to come back, for
what, an ideal, a cause? That's bull,
man, bull. That's a waste, man,
we're going to die for nothing.*

                   CHUCK

We did what we thought was right.

They stop to rest:

                    JOE

*I know, that's the point ... we were
wrong. It's pathological, Chuck. We
were sick ... we were suffering
from a terrible disease ... emotional
boredom. We knew that we had to
dedicate ourselves to something.
The thing we should've dedicated
ourselves to was life, not death ...
and that's what it was, Chuck ... a
death wish.*

Chuck looks up at Joe from the ground where he is
lying:

                   CHUCK

Give me a cigarette, Joe.

Joe lights a cigarette and puts it in Chuck's mouth:

                   CHUCK

                 (continuing)

*It's strange how strong man clings
to life, no matter how willing he
seems to throw it away.*

(CONTINUED)

48. (continued)

> JOE
>
> *For the wrong things, Chuck. You didn't come back to do anything necessary. We should've gone back home.*

> CHUCK
>
> *We shouldn't have come here in the first place, Joe. Things weren't really that bad after all, were they, Joe? That beer cellar near Hog's Head. Ah. I wish I had my stereo here, Joe, we could put on "The Charge of the Light Brigade"...*

Chuck starts humming the music:

> CHUCK
>
> *(continuing)*
>
> *What were we looking for?*

> JOE
>
> *We were looking for something to justify our useless lives. We weren't looking for anything, we were trying to lose ourselves.*

A dog sneaks into their hiding place and cowers on its belly, closer and closer:

> CHUCK
>
> *Look at that ... he's lonely and comes to us. Get lost, mutt, we're losers.*

The dog nuzzles up to Chuck and lies next to him.

(CONTINUED)

48. (continued)
    Chuck pets him:

> CHUCK
>
> *(continuing)*
>
> *That's one of the greatest feelings to have: a dog sleep next to you in front of a fire.*

> JOE
>
> *That's what I'm talking about. Those are the important things. We had to come to Africa to find out. When we get back, we'll enjoy those things again, Chuck. We'll raise hell again.*

Joe starts to break down:

> JOE
>
> *(continuing)*
>
> *Man, we'll enjoy it all ... Chuck? Chuck?*

Chuck's head is now slumped to the side, and the cigarette falls out of his mouth, while the dog licks his bloody hand:

> JOE
>
> *(continuing)*
>
> *Chuck? Don't leave me alone. Jesus. Don't leave me alone.*

Joe buries Chuck as best as he can in the tall grass. As a heavy rain begins to fall, Joe lifts his head while crying and screams out into the night, raising his fists to the sky. Joe pushes on.

(CONTINUED)

49. EXT.—VELD—DAWN   49.
After some narrow escapes when Joe comes close to
rebel forces, he comes up to a deserted plantation
house.

50. EXT.—PLANTATION HOUSE   50.
The heavy rainfall continues as Joe moves toward the
house, where he hopes to find shelter from the elements.

51. INT.—PLANTATION HOUSE   51.
In the dark shambles of the interior of what once was
obviously a home of luxury, Joe sees that the house is
empty except for the library, which is almost intact; the
volumes are now ruined by the rain coming in through
the broken ceiling. Joe turns around and finds himself
face to face with a LONE REBEL. Joe looks around quickly
to see if anyone else is present, then points his rifle at
the man. Joe can see that the rebel has taken shelter
in the house from the storm. Joe has the advantage,
for he is armed with several automatic weapons, while
the rebel has only a knife:

JOE

*I don't want trouble, just get out of
here . . .go . . .*

The rebel just stares at him:

JOE

(continuing)

Hell, you don't understand me.

LONE REBEL

(in Bantu)

(CONTINUED)

51. (continued)
    Why did you come here?

                    JOE

    *I don't understand you. I don't mean
    you any harm . . . just go.*

                 LONE REBEL

                 (in Bantu)

    *You wish to kill me, like you have
    done to all my people, but we will
    kick you into your grave.*

                    JOE

                (gesturing)

    *I don't understand . . . get out of
    here. Get your gear and go.*

Joe points to a bundle of things on the floor with the
muzzle of his rifle, at which time the rebel lunges at
him with his knife. The force of the blow carries the
rebel over the muzzle of the rifle, which goes off acci-
dentally. Joe's face and hands are splashed with
blood, which steams hot in the cool morning air. Joe
takes the rebel's bundle and goes through its contents.
He finds a book which he had read in college; he remembers, in flashbacks, his professor talking about
the book. For the first time he starts to understand the
book and what the professor had said. The book, *Vol
de Nuit,* a novel by Antoine de Saint-Exupéry, touches
Joe because, like the protagonist:

                PROFESSOR (V.O.)

    *. . . danger and near death had
    given him an appreciation of the
    simple things, a real love of life . . .*

52. EXT.—VELD—NIGHT   52.
Joe is working his way back to Salisbury and safety.

53. INT.—WILLOUGHBY'S OFFICE—DAY   53.
Willoughby, though surprised to see Joe, welcomes
him as a hero of sorts. After getting cleaned up and
fed, Joe is called to Willoughby's office:

WILLOUGHBY

(on the phone)

*. . . yes, Joe Bonner, the sole sur-
vivor of the Lampolo group of mercenaries . . . that's right . . . immediately. Is that understood?*

(hangs up)

*Mr. Bonner, from a grateful govern-
ment, you will receive full pay and
passage home to the States.*

JOE

(almost in a daze)

*You have to stop these recruiters
. . . someone should do something
. . . thank you.*

Joe stands up and shakes hands, then a SECRETARY escorts him out.

54. INT.—SHIP'S CABIN—EARLY EVENING   54.
Joe sits in his cabin and writes a wire to Mary back
home. As we see him leave the cabin, we begin to
HEAR the end of the WIRE:

                                            (CONTINUED)

54. (continued)

JOE (V.O.)

. . . and as I stood at the rail watching . . .

55. EXT.—SHIP'S DECK—EARLY EVENING   55.
Joe stands at the rail, watching the setting sun. African wild geese fly silhouetted against its redness:

JOE (V.O.)

. . . the wild geese flying overhead on their Night Flight, I thought of my Night Flight, which had brought me here and would take me home, and I realized that courage, real courage, is in fighting the peaceful battles of everyday existence.

THE END

Chapter 5

THE SHOOTING SCRIPT

APOLOGIA

The shooting script, as covered here, is a throwback to the earlier days of filmmaking. It is not used today in the industry other than, in a slightly different form, in the area of television. It is, however, useful in the study of filmmaking and directing.

Some of you may be total filmmakers in a small industrial in-house studio or hyphenated filmmakers—writer-directors like myself—and for you this form will provide essential knowledge. Even for those of you who are writers, familiarity with this form will improve awareness of all the filmic elements and enable you to write superior scripts.

The shooting script is an invaluable learning tool for the writer; I will go farther and say, as a filmmaker, that I value this form as a way of making my mistakes on paper, therefore saving time, which is money. The shooting script is helpful in maintaining control of the film, in predicting its outcome, and in bringing the film in on schedule. And one can still meet the unexpected and improvise—after all, it's only on paper.

Now that we have the screenplay in which the plot has been fully developed with all of its characters, locations, sets, and dialogue, we can introduce the most important element, the one which until now we have ignored: the camera. The shooting script will provide all of the camera directions and other technical information which the production crew needs.

The shooting script is written from the master scene script and is, in effect, an elaboration of it. The divisions by scenic headings presented in the screenplay are further subdivided into their individual shots. There are places in the scene which imply a shot. Words, phrases, and many times dialogue imply a cut or suggest a new shot.

Now let's take scene number one from the screenplay and see what shots are possible:

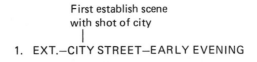

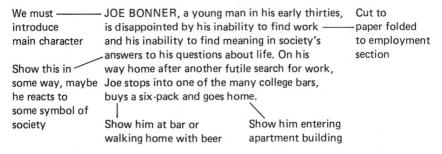

The *shot* is the building block of the script or film. It is the "word" of the filmic language. A shot is any one continuous, unedited piece of film. It can also be thought of as one *take*, being the time from when the camera is turned on until it is turned off.

Theoretically one could shoot an entire day, or indeed the entire film, without stopping, in which case it would still be one shot. A shooting script is composed of consecutively numbered shots. The shot supplies certain information to be used by the director and the crew to shoot the film.

In the following example I have labeled every part of the shot. The terms are defined below:

Shot Number: Used to identify the shot in the script breakdown and shooting schedule.

Scenic Heading: Gives the location of the action, whether it is inside or outside, and the relative time of day.

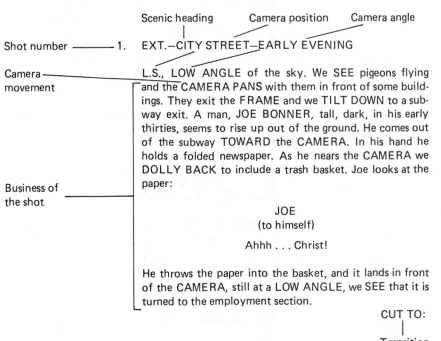

Camera Position: Tells the relative distance of subject to the camera. (See Figure 5-1.)

Business: Contains all of the descriptive material and visual imagery from the screenplay, sound notations, and camera movements. (For camera movements, see Figure 5-2.)

Dialogue: Contains all the speaking lines, narration, and dialogue notations. (For dialogue notations, see Figure 5-3.)

Transition: This last element of the shot tells how we intend to move from this shot to the next. (See Figure 5-4.)

EXTREME LONG SHOT (E.L.S.)

Used to show countryside skylines, and so on.

LONG SHOT (L.S.)

Full or total shot shows all of subject.

MEDIUM SHOT (M.S.)

Showing human figures from the knees or waist up.

CLOSE-UP (C.U.)

From the chest or shoulders up.

EXTREME CLOSE-UP (E.C.U.)

Also known as a DETAIL, it moves in on a small detail of the whole.

Figure 5-1

PAN left/right

Camera pivots side to side, horizontally.

TILT up/down

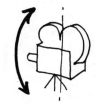

Camera pivots up and down, vertically.

DOLLY in/out

Camera on a wheeled vehicle called a dolly moves toward and away from subject. Sometimes ZOOM is used.

TRUCK SHOT

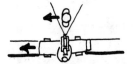

Camera moves on dolly along with subject.

CRANE SHOT

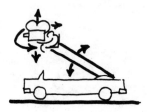

Camera mounted on a crane can move up and down and side to side at the same time.

Figure 5-2

NORMAL DIALOGUE

JOE
Hi, Mary.

OFF SCREEN (o.s.)

MARY (o.s.)
Hi, Joe. How are you?

VOICE OVER (V.O.)
Person thinks and we
hear thoughts.

JOE (V.O.)
She's really something
special.

A voice over the radio,
loudspeaker, telephone, etc.

MARY (V.O.)
In the coffee shop in an
hour.

Narrator or announcer,
the person is not seen.

NARRATOR (V.O.)
. . . and as the sun reflects
off the beautiful Lampolo
river.

Figure 5-3

CUT

The cut is the most used; it is the simple joining of two shots.

FADE

One shot fades out to black as the next shot fades in from black.

DISSOLVE

One shot fades out while the next fades in, and they overlap.

SPECIAL EFFECTS: These transitions are used only for special reasons, usually comic.

WIPE (horizontal/vertical/ iris/etc.)

One shot in some way moves over the next shot or pushes it out of the frame.

ZIP PAN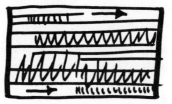

The camera pans so fast that it blurs the cut.

Figure 5-4

A few last points are worth mentioning: A character's name should be capitalized the first time he or she is introduced in the script. A rule of thumb says that one page of script equals one minute of screen time; thus, a two and a half hour film would be approximately 150 pages long. Finally, the following types of script directions should always be capitalized:

SCENIC HEADING

CAMERA POSITION

CAMERA MOVEMENT

DIALOGUE HEADING

TRANSITIONS

SOUND NOTES

In conclusion, the following chart shows how each element of the shot supplies information needed by the production staff.

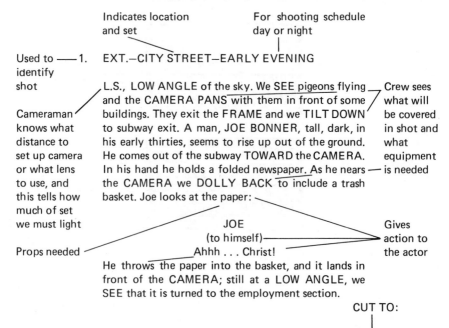

Indicates location
and set

For shooting schedule
day or night

Used to ——1.   EXT.–CITY STREET–EARLY EVENING
identify
shot

L.S., LOW ANGLE of the sky. We SEE pigeons flying — Crew sees
and the CAMERA PANS with them in front of some   what will
Cameraman   buildings. They exit the FRAME and we TILT DOWN   be covered
knows what   to subway exit. A man, JOE BONNER, tall, dark, in   in shot and
distance to   his early thirties, seems to rise up out of the ground.   what
set up camera   He comes out of the subway TOWARD the CAMERA.   equipment
or what lens   In his hand he holds a folded newspaper. As he nears — is needed
to use, and   the CAMERA we DOLLY BACK to include a trash
this tells how   basket. Joe looks at the paper:
much of set
we must light   JOE   Gives
                                  (to himself)———————— action to
Props needed ——   Ahhh . . . Christ!   the actor
He throws the paper into the basket, and it lands in
front of the CAMERA; still at a LOW ANGLE, we
SEE that it is turned to the employment section.

                                                    CUT TO:

                                               Tells editor and lab
                                               how we connect shots

Now let's return to our project and finish the shooting script. Take note that in the sample shooting script all the transitions marked CUT TO are eliminated except where they occur before scene changes. This style is in vogue in the industry. *We* do it in *this* book because such a transition is understood or implied in the script and because it saves space and makes the script more readable. The other transitional elements *are* included wherever they occur.

While going through the shooting script, I suggest that you turn back to the screenplay and keep checking it as you read along. In this way you will better understand the development of the shooting script from the screenplay. Comparing the two, you will see how the larger scenic units of the screenplay are expanded to their final form—the individual shots. It is a good idea to make a comparison of individual scenic units and concepts through their entire development in the script. For example, take the "death of Chuck" sequence and check its evolution from the beginning concept to the final shooting script.

Night Flight

SAMPLE SHOOTING SCRIPT

FADE IN:

1. EXT.—CITY STREET—EARLY EVENING   1.
   L.S., LOW ANGLE of the sky. We SEE pigeons flying and
   the CAMERA PANS with them in front of some buildings.
   They exit the FRAME and we TILT DOWN to a subway exit.
   A man, JOE BONNER, tall, dark, in his early thirties, seems
   to rise up out of the ground as he comes out of the
   subway TOWARD the CAMERA. In his hand he holds a
   newspaper. As he nears the CAMERA we DOLLY BACK to
   INCLUDE a trash basket. Joe looks at the paper:

JOE

(to himself)

Ahhh . . . Christ.

(CONTINUED)
115

1. (continued)

He throws the paper into the basket, and it lands in front of the CAMERA; still at a LOW ANGLE, we SEE that it is turned to the employment section.

DISSOLVE TO:

2. EXT.—CITY STREET—EARLY EVENING   2.

M.S. of Joe as he walks out of a bar, carrying a paper bag with a six-pack inside. The CAMERA TRUCKS with him as he walks along, past college-type bars and shops, the sidewalks crowded with people. A few people say hello, and he exchanges a few words with them.

DISSOLVE TO:

3. EXT.—APARTMENT BUILDING—EVENING   3.

C.U. of Joe as he stops in front of the building and looks up, then we—

CUT TO:

4. INT.—APARTMENT STAIRWELL—EVENING   4.

M.S. of Joe as he walks up the stairs. We HEAR the loud noise of his FOOTFALLS ECHOING in the stairwell. He stops on a landing and unlocks door.

CUT TO:

5. INT.—JOE'S APARTMENT   5.

L.S., the door opens and Joe enters into a dark, shabby room. CAMERA PANS with him to the refrigerator, he opens it, places six-pack inside.

6. M.S. of Joe: He sighs, and as the light of the open   6.
   door floods yellow over his face, we—

                                            CUT TO:

7. INT.—BAR—EVENING   7.
   A warm yellow light fills the bar, and we HEAR sounds
   of CLINKING GLASSES and LAUGHTER.

                                            CUT TO:

8. BACK TO JOE   8.
   C.U. of Joe as he reaches for a cold beer.

9. INT.—BAR   9.
   C.U. of Joe's hand as he reaches for paper bag with
   six-pack. CAMERA MOVES UP to the face of a barmaid
   named MARY. She is pretty, a brunette, in her late twenties:

                         MARY
                That'll be two-fifty.

10. C.U. of Joe: 10.

                          JOE
            Two-fifty? This better be good.

11. C.U. of Mary: 11.

MARY

*Well, if it's not, you can always bring
it back.*

She smiles at him.

CUT TO:

12. BACK TO JOE   12.
M.S. of Joe as he smiles, remembering her. He closes
the door of the refrigerator, and on the swing of the
door we—

DISSOLVE TO:

13. INT.—BAR—NIGHT   13.
M.S. of Joe, as the door swings open AWAY FROM CAM-
ERA. Joe enters, looks around.

14. C.U. of Joe, his face shows disappointment. As he   14.
turns, he bumps into MARY, the barmaid whom he was
looking for.

15. M.S. of the two, favoring Mary: 15.

MARY

*What's the matter, didn't you like the
beer?*

16. C.U. of Joe: 16.

JOE

(smiling)

Yeah, but I like you better.

17. M.S. of the two. She smiles back and goes about her   17.
business. CAMERA DOLLIES IN to a CLOSE-UP of Joe's face.
As he watches the retreating form of the attractive brunette, he forgets his problems and begins to enjoy
himself.

DISSOLVE TO:

18. M.S. of Joe at the bar talking to some people. The next   18.
time Mary comes close to Joe, he glances at her name
tag.

19. E.C.U. of her name tag, which reads MARY.   19.

20. M.S. of the two, favoring Joe: 20.

JOE

Mary . . . actually, I just hate to drink
alone.

21. C.U. of Mary: 21.

MARY

Poor baby.

22. C.U. of Joe: 22.

JOE

No, really.

23. C.U. of Mary: 23.

MARY

Well, you came to the right place.

She looks at the crush of people around them.

24. C.U. of Joe, as he follows her gaze around the bar.   24.

25. TWO SHOT as their eyes meet again.   25.

JOE

Yeah . . .

They both smile:

JOE

(continuing)

I guess I did.

She leaves, and as the evening progresses Joe keeps
Mary in view. After more eye games she comes close
again.

JOE

Look, I really do hate being alone.
How about a drink or something?

26. C.U. of Joe.   26.

27. C.U. of Mary: 27.

MARY
*I'll be off in a little, maybe a drink
... or something.*

She smiles at him mischievously and walks away.

28. C.U. of Joe, as he watches her walk away. He smiles   28.
and shakes his head.

DISSOLVE TO:

29. L.S. of booth: Joe is sitting with his drink as Mary   29.
walks up.

30. M.S., as Mary slides into the booth across from Joe.   30.

31. TWO SHOT, favoring Joe: 31.

JOE
*Hey, you're really super, thanks. My
name's Joe.*

32. C.U. of Mary: 32.

MARY
Joe what?

33. C.U. of Joe: 33.

JOE
Joe Bonner.

34. C.U. of Mary: 34.

MARY

Look, Joe, do you mind if we just walk a little? I have to get out of here before I suffocate.

35. C.U. of Joe: 35.

JOE
No problem, let's go.

36. M.S. of the two, as they get up to leave. CAMERA PANS   36.
with them as they exit, saying goodbye to a few people.

CUT TO:

37. EXT.—CITY STREET—NIGHT   37.
L.S. of the front of the bar, as Joe and Mary come out.
Once outside, a thin breeze seems to bring comfort to
them, erasing any tension which might have been
present. CAMERA TRUCKS with them as they walk.

DISSOLVE TO:

38. EXT.—CITY STREET—NIGHT   38.
M.S. of Joe and Mary as they walk along making small
talk.

DISSOLVE TO:

39. M.S. of the two as they pass a theatre.   39.

40. C.U. of the marquee, which reads *The Wild Bunch*.   40.

41. C.U. of Joe, looking wistfully.   41.

42. C.U. of the posters and stills in the showcase, all the   42.
blood-and-gut visuals from the movie.

43. M.S. of the two: 43.

JOE
How about catching a show?

44. C.U. of Mary: 44.

MARY
(annoyed)

What, that?

45. C.U. of Joe: 45.

JOE
What's wrong with that? That's a classic. It deals with camaraderie and courage . . .

46. C.U. of Mary: 46.

MARY
It deals with violence . . . and that's it.

47. C.U. of Joe, he starts to react.   47.

48. C.U. of Mary: 48.

MARY
The fact that it makes a show of dealing with greater issues makes it even worse.

49. C.U. of Joe: 49.

JOE
Look, I really like you . . .

50. C.U. of Mary: 50.

JOE
(continuing; o.s.)
Let's not let it ruin our evening . . .

51. C.U. of Joe: 51.

JOE
(continuing)
. . . before it even starts. Okay?

52. M.S. of the two. Mary smiles at him, and Joe touches   52.
her cheek:

MARY
Okay, Joe . . . okay.

(CONTINUED)

52. (continued)
   They continue to walk and do not notice as another young man comes up behind them.

53. M.S. of the young man, whom we will get to know as 53. CHUCK KING.

54. E.C.U. of Chuck's hand in his coat pocket. 54.

55. C.U. of Chuck, a grave expression on his face. 55.

56. M.S. of the three. CAMERA TRUCKS with Chuck as he 56. moves up close behind Joe and jams his hand into Joe's back.

57. E.C.U. of Chuck's face near Joe's ear: 57.

CHUCK

*All right, man, just hand over the
bread and no one will get hurt.*

58. C.U. of Mary. She is uncertain about what is happen- 58. ing and fixes her eyes on Joe for a clue.

59. M.S. of the three. Joe's hand starts easing into his 59. jacket pocket as though reaching for a gun.

60. C.U. of Mary, alarmed as she follows the movement. 60.

61. M.S. of the three. Joe pulls out his hand, which is 61. empty, and turns.

62. C.U. of Chuck's hand coming out of his pocket, also 62. empty.

63. M.S. of the three, as they point their fingers at each 63. other and make shooting noises.

64. C.U. of Mary in disbelief. 64.

65. M.S. of Joe and Chuck: 65.

CHUCK
Hi, Joe. How yah doin'?

66. C.U. of Joe: 66.

JOE
Okay, buddy. How are you?

67. C.U. of Chuck: 67.

CHUCK
Good.

68. M.S. of the three: 68.

JOE
Chuck, this is Mary.
He turns to Mary.

69. C.U. of Mary. She doesn't answer; she is irritated.   69.

70. C.U. of Chuck, obviously amused: 70.

CHUCK
Hi.

71. L.S. of the three, as they continue to walk. Mary is a 71.
little upset but relaxes again as they walk.

DISSOLVE TO:

72. M.S. of the three, as they walk. Chuck shows himself to 72.
be bright and articulate, and the level of conversation
is high. Joe and Chuck show themselves to be warm
and affable. The cool night air and the cheery twinkle
of neon put them in a festive mood.

DISSOLVE TO:

73. EXT.—BEER CELLAR—NIGHT   73.
M.S. of Joe, Mary, and Chuck, as they stop in front of
the establishment:

CHUCK
*How about a beer? They have an
imported dark beer that's out of this
world.*

JOE
Sounds good to me.
(to Mary)
What do you think?
Mary smiles, nods in consent.

74. C.U. of Mary: 74.

MARY

*I feel much better now. That sounds
good.*

CAMERA PULLS BACK as they enter the beer cellar.

DISSOLVE TO:

75. INT.—BEER CELLAR—NIGHT   75.
M.S. of Joe, Mary, and Chuck sitting at a booth. They
have the remains of sandwiches in front of them and a
half-filled pitcher of beer. The conversation has again
turned to violence:

JOE

*. . . I was trying to explain that vio-
lence is at the base of the American
cultural legacy of literature and film.
Even American history, itself, is
based on violence. The Americans
had to conquer first the land, then
the Indians, the English, the French,
the Spanish, the Mexicans . . .*

76. C.U. of Mary: 76.

MARY

*Okay . . . okay . . . I get the point. I
just don't believe it, and you seem
too intelligent to believe that.*

77. C.U. of Chuck: 77.

CHUCK

He's right. The trouble is that this country runs on a double standard. It admires physical strength, courage . . . all the classic male virtues, as long as it doesn't have to deal with them. When people need help, the call a cop, but when everything is cool, cops are vulgar and callous, to be avoided.

78. C.U. of Joe: 78.

JOE

Or in time of war everybody relies on the soldiers to save their bacon. They train them to kill and destroy; they are heroes and everybody loves them. But when the war is over, we try to forget them, we are embarrassed by them, we try to hide them.

79. C.U. of Mary: 79.

MARY

Hey! What is this? That may have been true in the past, but not today, not after Vietnam. Today, people are too aware of the realities. People know it's wrong to kill. There is no more flag-waving today, in peace or war.

80. C.U. of Chuck: 80.

CHUCK

*Nam was a fluke, it was cool to be
against it. But already people were
ready to go to Panama and kick
ass. Or listen to people on the
street. They want to go and get the
Arabs . . .*

                                    DISSOLVE TO:

81. M.S. of the three. As the evening progresses, Joe and 81.
Chuck become rowdy and start carrying on.

82. M.S. of a MAN sitting at the bar, beating his hands on 82.
the bar top as though it were a drum.

83. M.S. of Chuck, as he calls out to the man: 83.

CHUCK

*Hey. That's good. Why don't you try
that with your head.*

84. C.U. of the man, who glares at Chuck, and then turns 84.
back to his drink.

85. M.S. of the booth. They all laugh, but Mary is annoyed 85.
yet can't help smiling at the humor:

JOE

Come on, Chuck, let's pop the big-

                                              (CONTINUED)

85. (continued)

> *gest guy here and start some ac-*
> *tion.*

Joe throws a few mock punches, bobs and weaves in his chair.

86. C.U. of Chuck: 86.

CHUCK

> *Okay ... I'll tap him and you back*
> *me up.*

Chuck looks around.

87. L.S. of the crowd. CAMERA PANS across the people and 87. STOPS on a BIG GUY at the bar.

88. M.S. of the big guy at the bar. He has a crew cut and 88. a battered face.

89. C.U. of Chuck, looking at Joe, motioning to the man at 89. the bar.

90. C.U. of Mary: 90.

MARY

> *Come on, you guys are crazy. He's*
> *not bothering you. Besides, he looks*
> *like he could tear your head off.*

91. C.U. of Joe: 91.

> JOE
>
> *Are you kidding? Chuck'll knock him
> into the middle of next week.*

92. C.U. of Chuck, with a big smile on his face.   92.

93. C.U. of Joe: 93.

> JOE
>
> *(continuing)*
>
> *And if Chuck can't handle him, I'll
> be all over him like a fat rat in a
> cheese factory. I'll eat holes through
> him.*

94. C.U. of Chuck, laughing.   94.

95. C.U. of Joe: 95.

> JOE
>
> *(continuing)*
>
> *I'll be all over him like a baggy rain-
> coat.*

96. M.S. of the three, as they howl with laughter: 96.

> MARY
>
> *You two are like kids. You're too
> much.*

Meanwhile, in the booth behind them, four men who

(CONTINUED)

96. (continued)
have been overhearing the conversation begin making
comments about Joe and Chuck.

97. C.U. of one of the four men, who makes a funny noise. 97.

98. M.S. of Chuck, as he turns toward the men: 98.

CHUCK

You say something?

99. M.S. of the four men. They ignore Chuck. 99.

100. C.U. of Chuck: 100.

CHUCK

*Hey, slick ... I said, did you say
something?*

101. M.S. of Joe, as he motions Chuck down: 101.

JOE

Sit down, Chuck.

102. M.S. of Chuck: 102.

CHUCK

Don't worry ...

He turns back to the man.

103. C.U. of the first man, who is now serious: 103.

(CONTINUED)

103. (continued)

> 1st MAN
>
> *Yeah, I said . . .*

The man repeats the FUNNY NOISE, and the four of them laugh uncontrollably.

104. C.U. of Chuck, he starts to laugh.   104.

105. C.U. of Joe, pretending to look worried: 105.

> JOE
>
> *Chuck, the odds . . . leave them alone.*

106. M.S. of Chuck, as he turns again to the four men and 106. MIMICS their laughter:

> CHUCK
>
> *That's pretty funny, ace–almost as funny as your face.*

107. M.S. of the four, they stop laughing.   107

108. C.U. of Joe: 108

> JOE
>
> *(loud)*
>
> *Chuck, the odds aren't fair . . .*

109. M.S. of the other men, who have risen and start to sit 109. again.

110. C.U. of Joe: 110.

JOE
There's only four of them, sit down.

111. L.S. of the four men, they jump up out of their seats. 111.

112. C.U. of Mary, flabbergasted.   112.

113. C.U. of Chuck, laughing.   113.

114. M.S. of Joe, Mary, and Chuck. Mary jumps out of the 114.
     booth:

MARY
Let's get out of here before some-
thing happens . . . please.
She begins to leave, trying to pull Joe and Chuck with
her.

115. M.S. of the four men, who are holding their ground, 115.
     watching the three as they leave:

2nd MAN
Tasty . . . nice . . . I'd like to . . .
The rest of his COMMENT is UNINTELLIGIBLE.

116. M.S. of the three nearing the door. Mary looks back 116.
     and Joe yells over his shoulder, as she pushes him out
     the door:

(CONTINUED)

116. (continued)

> JOE
>
> *It'd be too crowded ...*

117. M.S. of the four men. The second man starts forward 117.
   again.

118. C.U. of Joe, just as he disappears out the door: 118.

> JOE
>
> *(continuing)*
>
> *... there's one ass in there already.*

119. L.S. of the four men, as they start to run after Joe.   119.

120. **EXT.—BEER CELLAR—NIGHT**   120.
   L.S., the front door bursts open and Joe, Mary, and
   Chuck run out and down the street.

121. M.S. of the three, as they run away from the bar, 121.
   laughing.

122. L.S. of the three, now they slow down and laugh, out of 122.
   breath.

123. M.S. of the three. They sit down on a stoop to rest.   123.

124. C.U. of Chuck: 124.

CHUCK
Listen, I gotta split . . . see you later.

125. C.U. of Joe: 125.

JOE
Okay, buddy.

126. C.U. of Chuck and Mary: 126.

CHUCK
I really enjoyed meeting you. Give Joe a chance, he's really a hell of a guy.

127. M.S., Chuck moves off down the street, and Joe turns 127. to Mary. CAMERA DOLLIES IN SLOWLY:

JOE
Look, I hope that I haven't scared you away tonight . . . we were just having some fun.

128. C.U. of Mary, she stares at him for a while.   128.

129. C.U. of Joe.   129.

130. C.U. of Mary.   130.

MARY
I like what I think I see inside of you

(CONTINUED)

130. (continued)
> *... and I think I'd like to see more.*
> *Please call me some time at the*
> *bar.*

131. L.S. She places her hand on his cheek and kisses him 131.
softly, then she quickly walks away down the street.

FADE OUT:

FADE IN:

132. EXT.—CITY STREET—DAY 132.
L.S. Joe is walking along the street with an armful of
groceries and runs into Mary.

133. M.S. of Joe and Mary: 133.

MARY

Hi, Joe.

JOE

Hi, you sure look good today ...
tasty.

134. C.U. of Mary: 134.

MARY

(smiles)

Oh, please don't start.

135. M.S. They laugh and start walking together. HEAD-ON 135.

(CONTINUED)

135. (continued)
SHOT, CAMERA DOLLIES BACK with them as they walk:

JOE
How have you been?

MARY
Good, Joe.

JOE
It's really good to see you, Mary.
Joe stops walking and turns to Mary.

136. C.U. of Joe: 136.

JOE
Listen, how about coming over to my place? I just bought all these good things, and I'll cook you the best gourmet lunch you have ever had.

137. C.U. of Mary: 137.

MARY
That sounds great, Joe ... let's go.

138. M.S. She takes his arm and they go.   138.

DISSOLVE TO:

139. INT.—JOE'S APARTMENT—DAY   139.
     L.S. The darkness of the apartment is pierced by the
     light from the open door. Joe and Mary walk into the
     apartment.

140. M.S. of Mary, as she does a double take. CAMERA PANS 140.
     with her as she looks around the apartment. There is a
     great clutter of books, movie posters from western, po-
     lice, and adventure films, all dealing with the glorifica-
     tion of war and violence. The walls are covered with
     guns and knives of every description.

141. C.U. of Mary: 141.

                       MARY
            My God! You have an arsenal here.
            What are you expecting, a war?

142. C.U. of Joe: 142.

                        JOE
            I wish.

143. C.U. of Mary, shocked: 143.

                       MARY
            What?

144. C.U. of Joe: 144.

                        JOE
            Just kidding . . . but I really do crave

(CONTINUED)

144. (continued)

> *adventure. I know it's trite and over-stated, but I wish I had been born earlier.*
>
> (assumes a British accent)
>
> *When men were men, by Jove, Bal-aclava, the thin red line, and all that.*

145. C.U. of Mary: 145.

MARY

You're crazy, I swear.

146. M.S. She grabs his face in her hands, Joe grabs her 146.
and kisses her, she responds.

147. L.S. She breaks away and moves into the kitchen: 147.

MARY

You're supposed to be cooking.

Joe goes after her into the kitchen.

148. M.S. as he gives her little kisses on the back of her 148.
neck:

JOE

I am, honey, I am.

She turns into his arms and they stagger back against
the stove.

149. C.U. They begin to laugh.   149.

DISSOLVE TO:

150. M.S. of Joe, as he cooks in the foreground, Mary is in 150.
     the background making drinks. She gives him his drink
     and walks around the apartment.

151. M.S. of Mary, drink in hand, looking at his books: 151.

>   MARY
> *Have you read these books or are*
> *they here just for show?*

152. C.U. of Joe, he stops setting the table and stares at 152.
     her:

>   JOE
> *Yes, I've read them, all of them.*

153. C.U. of Mary: 153.

>   MARY
> *You've read these books and you*
> *can still carry on like a psychotic*
> *boy scout? Macho man.*

154. M.S. She walks to him: 154.

>   MARY
>   *(continuing)*
> *All that business about the call of*
> *adventure ... it's all romantic bull.*
> *Don't you see that?*

(CONTINUED)

JOE

*It's not bull . . . the order of things is
an order which we impose on it.*

155. C.U. of Mary: 155.

MARY

I don't understand.

156. M.S. Joe finishes bringing the food to the table: 156.

JOE

*You imply that the romantic view is
not realistic, that it's idealistic or
pathological . . . What I'm saying is
that man imposes his own order on
things, his own view and code of
ethics which he must live by. That is
reality.*

She moves close to him and places a finger on his
lips:

MARY

*Let's eat and then in bed you can
tell me more of Man and the nature
of things.*

157. C.U. of Joe.   157.

158. C.U. of Mary.   158.

FADE OUT:

FADE IN:

159. INT.—STAIRWELL OF JOE'S APARTMENT HOUSE—
MORNING   159.
L.S., LOW ANGLE UP TOWARD window at head of stairs. The
early morning sun streams in heavy shafts from the
window on the landing. Dust particles float like smoke
through the sunlight. Legs creep up the stairs, the CAM-
ERA MOVES WITH HIM as he gets close to Joe's door. The
CAMERA TILTS UP to show a gun in the man's hand. The
man lifts the gun and knocks on the door with the gun
barrel.

160. INT.—JOE'S APARTMENT   160.
C.U. of Joe, asleep. He hears the KNOCKING at the door
and opens his eyes.

161. M.S. Joe reaches into the night stand.   161.

162. E.C.U. of Joe's hand reaching for gun.   162.

163. L.S. Joe, in his shorts, goes to the door.   163.

164. C.U. of Joe: 164.

                          JOE ·
              Who is it?

165. INT.—HALLWAY   165.
C.U. of thumb cocking the hammer of the gun, with a loud CLICK. The hand moves up and the CAMERA TILTS UP with it to reveal Chuck:

CHUCK

Chuck . . . I got a present for you.

166. BACK TO JOE   166.
E.C.U. of Joe's hand unlocking the door quietly.

167. M.S. of Joe, as he moves behind the cover of a book- 167.
case:

JOE

It's open, come on in.

168. L.S. Chuck kicks the door open and, as he enters, 168.
both he and Joe take mock shots at each other, as they scream and make shooting noises.

169. M.S. They both laugh and put the guns down: 169.

CHUCK

Top of the morn', old bean.
(then)

Any coffee?

JOE

And the rest of the day to you.

170. CAMERA PANS with Joe as he goes to the stove and 170. puts on some coffee:

JOE
(continuing)

Come on, Chuck, let's go ... let's pack up and get the hell out of here. Let's go hunt bandits in Bolivia, or Sardinia. You know they still have bandits in the mountains there?

CAMERA PANS with him back to Chuck.

171. C.U. of Chuck: 171.

CHUCK

Mexico ... not too long ago a small town in Mexico was having problems ...

172. M.S. of Chuck. CAMERA PANS with him as he moves 172. to the coffee:

CHUCK
(continuing)

... with bandits, you know. They took over the whole town.

Chuck fixes himself a cup of coffee:

CHUCK
(continuing)

Well, two Americans went down as

(CONTINUED)

172. (continued)

> *bounty hunters . . . like in the West,*
> *you know . . .*

CAMERA PANS BACK with him to Joe:

CHUCK

> *. . . and they had a big shoot-out in*
> *the middle of the town, killed them*
> *all . . . unbelievable. Collected their*
> *bounty and came back like fat cats.*

173. C.U. of Joe, as he drinks his coffee: 173.

JOE

> *That sounds great. Come on, let's*
> *do it. Let's sell everything and get a*
> *jeep . . . pack up the guns and*
> *go. . . . Come on.*

174. M.S. of both, as Chuck leans toward Joe: 174.

CHUCK

> *You're kidding, I'm not. I really*
> *would do it.*

175. C.U. of Chuck: 175.

CHUCK

(continuing)

> *You weren't in Nam, I was. The bull*
> *is hard to take, you know—the disci-*
> *pline, the power-tripping officers*
> *and so on. But when you're on your*
> *own, maybe a mercenary, you*

(CONTINUED)

175. (continued)

> *know, a soldier of fortune, that's different.*

176. C.U. of Joe: 176.

JOE

(mock seriousness)

And we're stuck here, busting a few heads in a bar, target shooting on Saturdays . . .

177. C.U. of Chuck: 177.

CHUCK

Bust a few heads . . . What, mere mortals? Bring us giants.

CAMERA DOLLIES BACK to M.S. to INCLUDE Joe, as they stand up and pose.

DISSOLVE TO:

178. L.S. Later, after much drinking, the two are lying on the 178. floor with their drinks and a plate of cold chicken. Classical music fills the air. CAMERA PANS with them as they go to the guns and begin arming themselves.

179. M.S. of the two, as they strap on holsters and knives. 179.

180. C.U. of Joe: 180.

(CONTINUED)

180. (continued)

JOE

Let's take a picture.

He holds up a camera and looks at it; there are a few shots left.

181. M.S. They set up the camera on a table and run back to pose. 181.

182. E.C.U. of the camera. 182.

183. They pose as the flash goes off. 183.

FADE OUT:

FADE IN:

184. L.S. The apartment is in shambles and Joe is asleep. The PHONE RINGS. 184.

185. C.U., LOW ANGLE of the telephone in the foreground. Joe reaches for the phone: 185.

JOE

Hello.

MARY (V.O.)

Good morning . . . Joe?

JOE

Good morning, honey. How are you?

186. INT.—MARY'S APARTMENT   186.
     C.U. of Mary:

MARY
Joe, let's do something today. It's such a gloomy day . . . it's raining and I'm lonely. I'd like very much to see you.

187. C.U. of Joe: 187.

JOE
Sure . . . How about breakfast?

(scratches head in pain)

Well, coffee anyway . . . downstairs in the coffee shop, in about an hour. Okay? Bye.

188. C.U. of Mary: 188.

MARY
See you then, Joe . . . I love you.

DISSOLVE TO:

189. EXT.—COFFEE SHOP—MORNING   189.
     L.S. of coffee shop window. It is raining and Joe is sitting alone in front of window.

DISSOLVE TO:

190. INT.—COFFEE SHOP   190.
     M.S. of Joe. A heavy rain is falling outside the window

190. (continued)
in front of which Joe sits with Mary. They are enjoying themselves, chatting softly, almost unintelligibly, in the pleasant, warm interior of the coffee shop. In the distance through the window, we SEE Chuck approaching, running to escape the rain. Chuck enters the door near their table, sits down.

191. C.U. of Chuck: 191.

CHUCK

Hi, folks.

192. M.S. of the three: 192.

CHUCK

(continuing)

Joe . . . you're gonna die.

He pulls a magazine out of his jacket and leafs through it:

CHUCK

(continuing)

Look at this.

He gives the magazine to Joe and indicates something with his finger.

193. C.U. of Joe, smiling and shaking his head. He looks 193.
up:

JOE

That's too much . . . I don't believe it.

194. C.U. of Mary: 194.

MARY

What is it?

195. M.S. of the three: 195.

JOE

It's an ad for mercenaries.

MARY

What?

JOE

*Yeah. An ad for mercenaries–to go
to Rhodesia.*

Mary gets upset:

CHUCK

Excellent pay, it says.

196. C.U. of Mary: 196.

MARY

*That's not funny, Joe ... They
shouldn't allow things like that to be
published.*

197. C.U. of Chuck: 197.

CHUCK

Well, they did.

198. C.U. of Joe, as he smiles.   198.

199. C.U. of Mary: 199.

MARY
*Those poor people over there are
fighting for their political and eco-
nomical life against racism at its
most savage. . . .*

200. C.U. of Joe: 200.

JOE
They're just a bunch of bandits too.

201. C.U. of Mary: 201.

MARY
*Bandits? They've been under the
heel of the whites for too long . . .
they've had enough.*

202. C.U. of Chuck, now getting a little hot: 202.

CHUCK
*Bull. They're communists, trouble-
makers, and terrorists.*

203. C.U. of Joe: 203.

JOE

Communists, what the hell are communists? They are patriots fighting for their independence. Come on, Chuck, we'd do the same thing. We did the same thing in our revolution.

204. M.S. of the three. Mary stands up: 204.

MARY

(angry)

Look, Joe, I'm going up to the apartment.

JOE

Mary, come on.

But she leaves:

CHUCK

Let her go, she'll calm down. Look, I'm sorry, Joe . . . I'm just tired of bleeding hearts.

205. C.U. of Joe: 205.

JOE

Cool it, Chuck, just cool it, man. She's a great chick and I don't want to hurt her. Okay?

206. M.S. of the two: 206.

> CHUCK
>
> *Okay.*

They sit in silence:

> CHUCK
>
> *(continuing)*
>
> *I sent a letter.*

> JOE
>
> *What letter? What the hell are you talking about?*

207. C.U. of Chuck: 207.

> CHUCK
>
> *I answered the ad.*

He taps the magazine.

208. C.U. of Joe: 208.

> JOE
>
> *You're crazy, man. You're out of your mind.*
>
> *(gets up)*
>
> *I'm leaving, I'm going up.*

He turns to leave.

209. C.U. of Chuck: 209.

> CHUCK
>
> *Just think about it, Joe.*

210. M.S. of Joe, as he walks out the door.   210.

211. C.U. of Chuck: 211.

CHUCK

Just think about it.

FADE OUT:

FADE IN:

212. INT.—JOE'S APARTMENT   212.
M.S., the door opens and Joe, soaking wet from the
rain, walks in. He looks around:

JOE

Mary?

He sees that she is not there and throws his jacket on
floor.

JOE

(continuing)

Damn it.

FADE TO:

213. EXT.—CITY STREET—NIGHT   213.
L.S. Joe is walking and Chuck comes up to him:

CHUCK

Hi, Joe . . . How's it goin'?

(CONTINUED)

213. (continued)

JOE

Good. You?

CHUCK

Seen Mary since the coffee shop?

JOE

No. Not for a week.

214. C.U. of Chuck: 214.

CHUCK

Joe . . . look, I'm sorry if I . . .

215. C.U. of Joe: 215.

Joe

That's okay, don't worry about it.

216. C.U. of Chuck: 216.

CHUCK

No, really I . . .

217. C.U. of Joe: 217.

JOE

*Don't worry about it . . . If that's all it
took to chase her away, she wasn't
worth it.*

218. M.S. of the two, as they continue walking in silence: 218.

CHUCK
I got an answer.

JOE
Answer to what?

CHUCK
From the mercenary recruiters.

JOE
What did they say?

CHUCK
There's a reception at a big hotel in town. Should be good, free booze and food . . . I'm going. Want to go?

219. C.U. of Joe: 219.

JOE
Why not, can't dance.

FADE OUT:

FADE IN:

220. EXT.—HOTEL—NIGHT   220.
L.S. to establish. It is a hot night. Joe and Chuck walk up to the hotel entrance, a thin veil of perspiration on their faces.

221. **INT.—HOTEL LOBBY**   221.
     M.S. of Joe and Chuck as they enter. They sigh in re-
     lief as the air conditioning hits them:

                          JOE
            Ah, man, that feels good.

222. C.U. of Chuck: 222.

                         CHUCK
            I'm hungry. I hope they have some-
            thing good to eat.
     CAMERA PANS with them as they walk to the elevators.
     They wait in silence. The door opens, they get in.

223. **INT.—ELEVATOR**   223.
     M.S. of the two:

                          JOE
            Where the hell is this thing?

                         CHUCK
            (checks slip of paper)
            409 Club . . . reception room 1037.
     The doors open on the tenth floor.

224. **INT.—CORRIDOR**   224.
     M.S. as they come off the elevator;

                          JOE
            I really feel stupid.
                                              (CONTINUED)

224. (continued)

CHUCK

That's okay, you look stupid too.

DISSOLVE TO:

225. INT.—HOTEL SUITE   225.
M.S. of Joe and Chuck as they enter. The suite is plush. CAMERA PANS the suite. The room is full of people. There are a few men in Rhodesian military uniforms and a conspicuous overabundance of sexy women in revealing evening clothes. In the center of the room is a long table covered with a fine selection of canapés and hors d'oeuvres, all clustered around a large silver tray full of wine glasses, which are constantly replenished by an attendant.

226. C.U. of Chuck: 226.

CHUCK

Man, look at that spread.

227. C.U. of Joe, looking at a woman: 227.

JOE

Yeah . . . look at that spread.

228. M.S. of the woman, sexy.   228.

229. M.S. of the two: 229.

CHUCK

I'm talking about the food, Joe.

(CONTINUED)

229. (continued)

JOE

They went to a lot of trouble to im-press us.

CHUCK

Yes, and they did a good job, I'm impressed.

JOE

What I mean is: this is all window dressing, man.

CAMERA PANS with them as they help themselves to the food.

230. C.U. of Chuck: 230.

CHUCK

I know that, but the food is real, and the chicks are too.

231. C.U. of Joe: 231.

JOE

Wrong, buddy boy, the chicks are unreal.

232. L.S. over Joe's shoulder of a beautiful woman, WENDY, 232. in a most revealing outfit, approaching the two men. CAMERA PULLS BACK to SHOW all three:

WENDY

Hi. How are you fellows tonight?

(CONTINUED)

232. (continued)

CHUCK

(eyeing her)

Not as good as you.

JOE

Fine.

WENDY

*Where are your name tags? I'm
Wendy.*

JOE

I'm Joe Bonner.

He reaches out to shake her hand:

CHUCK

(reaches for sandwich)

I'm hungry, excuse me.

Chuck moves out of the FRAME.

233. C.U. of Joe: 233.

JOE

*You'll have to excuse my friend,
Wendy ... What he lacks in man-
ners, he makes up for in candor,
which is not a bad trade.*

234. M.S. of Joe and Wendy. CAMERA TRUCKS with them as   234.
they move to a table where two men, one in a Rhodesian military uniform, MAJOR RHODES, and the other, FRANK
THORTON, a tall, good-looking man in an expensive dark

(CONTINUED)

234. (continued)
suit, are talking to each other. On the table is a selection of literature:

WENDY

Major Rhodes . . . Frank Thorton . . .
this is Joe Bonner.

MAJOR

How do you do, Mr. Bonner.

THORTON

Hi, Joe.
Thorton extends his large hand and almost crushes the smaller man's fingers in the handshake.

235. E.C.U. of handshake.   235.

236. C.U. of Joe's face, a slight flinch in his eyes.   236.

237. C.U. of Thorton. The man's thin, cruel smile just barely 237.
hides a less agreeable disposition given away by the glint of his cold blue eyes:

THORTON

Excuse me, Joe, I have to break . . .
just five.

238. M.S. of Joe, flexing his fingers: 238.

JOE

You already did.

(CONTINUED)

238. (continued)
He smiles at Thorton who sharply turns and moves
away with Wendy . . .

239. C.U. of Thorton . . . but not before clenching his jaw 239.
muscles and shooting Joe a sidelong glance that
opens, for a moment, that special window behind
everyone's eyes.

240. M.S. of Joe, turning to Chuck as he comes up with two 240.
drinks:

                         JOE
            That bastard about broke my hand
            . . . No sense of humor either.

                                        DISSOLVE TO:

241. **MONTAGE OF SHOTS**   241.
As the evening progresses Joe and Chuck become
more drunk. While still in control of themselves, they
begin to be sucked in by the power politics of the recruiters. They show films of the latest equipment being
used by mercenaries in Rhodesia, and the new, well-
equipped facilities of the Rhodesian camps and bases.

DISSOLVE TO:

242. M.S. of the Major: 242.

                        MAJOR
            . . . of course this will mean nothing
            to most of you until you get to the

(CONTINUED)

242. (continued)

> *front. What will interest you is the pecuniary remuneration.*

243. MAJOR'S POV (point of view) of the men. There are some 243. puzzled looks and some "Huhs" and "Whats" from the men.

244. C.U. of the Major: 244.

MAJOR
(continuing)
Money, my lads . . . money.

There is a mixture of LAUGHTER and APPLAUSE:

MAJOR
(continuing)
For the signing of our One Tour of Duty *contact, each recruit will receive nineteen thousand Rhodesian dollars, or approximately thirty thousand U.S. dollars.*

The men WHISTLE and APPLAUD:

MAJOR
(continuing)
Thank you. Mr. Thorton and I are willing to answer your questions.

245. M.S. of Joe and Chuck, looking at each other, thinking: 245.

> CHUCK
>
> *That's not bad, old bean. Thirty thousand bucks.*

> JOE
>
> *No . . . but it's no picnic for Christ's sake.*
>
> *(takes sip of drink)*
>
> *It's still war, damn it.*

> CHUCK
>
> *What the hell are you mumbling about? Come on, let's go.*

246. C.U. of Joe: 246.

> JOE
>
> *Go where?*

247. C.U. of Chuck: 247.

> CHUCK
>
> *And sign the contracts . . . Come on, you still can change your mind up until the time you leave London. You heard him, come on, let's go.*

248. L.S. of the two, as they get in line to sign the contract: 248.

> JOE
>
> *I still don't like it . . .*

(CONTINUED)

248. (continued)

CHUCK

Look, you went to school to write.
This will give you something to write
about. Right? Right.

249. M.S. of the two: 249.

CHUCK

(continuing)

Come on, you lazy bastard.

JOE

I'm coming, damn it, I'm coming.

FADE OUT:

FADE IN:

250. INT.—JOE'S APARTMENT—NIGHT   250.
Joe lets himself into the apartment amid great noise
and grumbling:

JOE

The Federales always lose ... the
rebels win everytime ...

MARY (o.s.)

What are you mumbling about?

Joe spins around.

251. M.S. of Mary in bed. She sleepily rubs her eyes.   251.

252. C.U. of Joe: 252.

JOE

*Mary . . . I thought I'd never see you
again.*

Joe is really feeling the booze:

JOE

(continuing)

I'm glad you came back.

253. M.S. of Joe. CAMERA PANS with him to the bed; he fum- 253.
bles with her:

JOE

I love you, Mary.

CAMERA MOVES IN SLOWLY:

JOE

(continuing)

*Really, Mary, I'm so glad . . . I didn't
think . . .*

Joe passes out in her arms.

FADE OUT:

FADE IN:

254. INT.—JOE'S APARTMENT—MORNING   254.

LOW ANGLE across Joe's sleeping form to the stove
where Mary is cooking. She is only wearing a pajama
top. Joe awakens to the sound and smell of bacon and

(CONTINUED)

254. (continued)
    eggs cooking. Joe rubs his head and lights a ciga-
    rette. He glances at her and sulks for a while, then
    gets out of bed and goes to her.

255. REVERSE ANGLE past Mary as Joe comes to her and gives 255.
    her a kiss. He looks disturbed:

                    MARY

        Joe, I'm going to move in here and
        take care of you. I'm sorry I got up-
        set . . . I wasn't fair to you.

    Joe begins milling about nervously:

                    JOE

        Mary, I . . .

                    MARY

        You don't have to say anything, I
        know . . .

256. C.U. of Joe: 256.

                    JOE

                (angry)

        You don't know anything. You don't
        know anything.

257. C.U. of Mary: 257.

                    MARY
        What's wrong?

258. C.U. of Joe: 258.

JOE

I signed . . .

259. C.U. of Mary: 259.

MARY

Signed what? What are you talking about?

260. C.U. of Joe: 260.

JOE

I'm talking about you and me . . . I signed a contract to go to Rhodesia.

261. C.U. of Mary, looking incredulous: 261.

MARY

What? You what?

262. M.S. as she rushes to him and starts slapping him 262. across his face:

MARY

(continuing)

You what? You stupid jerk.

He tries to settle her down:

(CONTINUED)

262. (continued)

> JOE
>
> *Calm down. It's not the end of the world, for God's sake.*

263. C.U. of Mary. She stops fighting and stares at him: 263.

> MARY
>
> *You really don't see, do you? You really don't see what you're doing, do you?*

264. C.U. of Joe: 264.

> JOE
>
> *I'll be back in time. If you really care, it'll hold.*

265. M.S. of Joe pacing around nervously: 265.

> JOE
>
> *I've got to do something. Don't you understand? I've had nothing but bad luck ... I've got to turn it around. I'm underqualified for the good jobs and overqualified for the bad ones.*

> MARY
>
> *Joe, I ...*

> JOE
>
> *You want to hear something funny? Huh? Do you?*

(CONTINUED)

265. (continued)

MARY

Joe, please . . .

266. C.U. of Joe: 266.

JOE

*I was turned down at a hot dog
stand . . . Do you hear me?*

267. M.S. of Joe, begins to cry: 267.

JOE

(continuing)

*I stood there and the guy told me
that I couldn't handle selling hot
dogs.*

Joe slams his fist on the table:

JOE

(continuing)

*He told me that I was not the type
they needed . . . not dynamic
enough to . . .*

(punches wall)

sell hot dogs.

He breaks down, and she runs to him and holds him in
her arms:

MARY

*You'll make it, Joe. You will, and if
you don't, it doesn't matter. You just*

(CONTINUED)

267. (continued)

keep trying ... The important thing is that you keep trying, that is what life is all about, Joe ... that is the meaning behind it all. That's the secret that women know.

268. C.U. of Joe: 268.

JOE

I know, but it's hard to settle for less than the top. Everyday, wherever you go, you are surrounded by plenty ... you know, every magazine, commercial, everything shows beautiful people in beautiful places, surrounded by expensive things, enjoying themselves. We are conditioned to want those things, damn it. But they don't supply us with any means of obtaining them.

269. C.U. of Mary: 269,

MARY

Honey, please ...

270. C.U. of Joe: 270.

JOE

No, let me finish. Today, without money, you're nothing ... and it's a fact of life. Everybody can't be a millionaire, but they make everybody

(CONTINUED)

270. (continued)

> want *it, and that's the crime . . . I*
> *want it, and I'm going to get it, and*
> *nothing is going to stop me . . .*
> *nothing.*

FADE OUT:

FADE IN:

271. EXT.—VETS CLUB—NIGHT   271.
On an unseasonably cold night, Joe and Chuck walk
along the street carrying duffle bags and stop in front
of the club. The club is in a run-down area of the city.
A drizzle begins to fall on them. As they talk, a few
more men begin to filter in.

272. M.S. of the two: 272.

JOE

Well, I hope we didn't make a mis-
take.

CHUCK

What mistake? We haven't even
started yet. There will be plenty of
time for mistakes once we get there.

JOE

I don't know . . . it's just a feeling, I
guess.

273. L.S. of an OLD MAN, who comes out of the club and 273.
motions to the men as a bus pulls up:

(CONTINUED)

273. (continued)

OLD MAN

Okay, let's go, come on, everybody,
in the bus.

JOE

I'm coming.

OLD MAN

Yeah, so's Christmas.

Everybody laughs and starts boarding the bus.

DISSOLVE TO:

274. INT.—BUS—NIGHT   274.
C.U. of Joe and Chuck, seated in the front row. The
bus is now moving out of the city:

JOE

When do we get to the airport?

CHUCK

I'm not sure, but we are suppose' to
take off at one thirty this morning.

CAMERA MOVES IN on Joe as he lights a cigarette and
stares out the window at the skyline.

275. C.U. of window. Joe's reflection in the window mixed 275.
with the city lights seen in the distance through his reflection gives him a feeling of vagueness.

276. C.U. of Joe. Somehow his transparent face on the rain- 276.
covered glass bothers him; it seems to imply a lack of
substance, that he doesn't exist anymore, that he is

(CONTINUED)

276. (continued)
just a shadow. CAMERA starts to TURN and ROTATE around him to an over-the-shoulder shot of the window.

277. L.S. of the window, the CAMERA MOVES IN to a CLOSE-UP. 277.

278. C.U. of Joe. As an intimation of doom washes over 278. Joe, the noise of the men in the bus fades from his consciousness, replaced by an almost thundering silence, which becomes . . .

279. C.U. of the window as the CAMERA MOVES IN.   279.
. . . the ROAR of AIRPLANE ENGINES. The reflection in the windown screams back at him—a terrible, soundless scream.

CUT TO:

280. INT.—PLANE—NIGHT   280.
The interior of the plane is spartan, only metal seats and no comforts. The ROAR of the ENGINES fades into the sound of Thorton's voice screaming at the men.

281. C.U. of Chuck: 281.

CHUCK

(lighting a pipe)

*Thorton's a real s.o.b. I think we are
in for trouble with him. I think we're
all in trouble.*

282. C.U. of Joe: 282.

JOE
*If this is an example of the kind of
equipment supplied by this bunch,
we're in big trouble.*

283. C.U. of Chuck: 283.

CHUCK
*It's not that bad. What the hell did
you expect?*

284. C.U. of Joe: 284.

I don't know myself.
Joe looks up.

285. L.S. of Thorton, coming up the aisle.   285.

286. M.S. of Joe and Thorton, as the recruiter passes: 286.

JOE
*Frank, is there anything to drink in
here? I'm . . .*

THORTON
*What the hell do you think this is,
Bonner? This ain't no friggin' cham-
pagne flight.*

The other men start laughing, and Thorton starts to
walk away.

287. M.S. of Joe and Chuck, looking at each other. Joe 287.
glances down at something.

288. E.C.U. of Joe's duffel bag.   288.

289. L.S. of the three men. Chuck pushes the duffel bag out 289.
into the aisle with his foot:

JOE
Hey, sorry I asked.

Thorton, turned toward Joe, trips over the bag and falls
flat on his face. The men roar in laughter.

290. M.S. of Thorton, as he gets up and rushes Joe: 290.

THORTON
You little . . .

He grabs Joe by the front of his shirt and pulls him out
of his seat. Joe breaks his hold and punches him in
the face.

291. C.U. of Thorton, as he staggers back and touches the 291.
blood on his lips. He grins, then—

292. L.S. of Thorton, as he goes for Joe. The COPILOT comes 292.
out of the cockpit.

293. C.U. of the copilot: 293.

COPILOT

(angry)

*Thorton! I won't have brawling on
my plane. Do you understand?*

(then)

Willoughby's on the wire.

294. C.U. of Thorton, glaring at the copilot: 294.

THORTON

Okay, mate . . . I'm coming.

295. M.S. of the copilot, as he goes back into the cockpit. 295.
Thorton follows, stopping at the door:

THORTON

Later, Bonner . . . later.

FADE OUT:

FADE IN:

296. INT.—HOTEL ROOM IN LONDON—EARLY EVENING 296.
The last rays of the sun stream into the otherwise dim
interior of the room, illuminating the sleeping forms of
Joe and Chuck. The PHONE RINGS:

297. C.U. of Chuck, awakening to the phone. He slowly 297.
reaches for it in his sleep:

(CONTINUED)

297. (continued)

> CHUCK
>
> *Hello . . . Yeah? Okay . . . in half an*
> *hour? Okay. Yeah . . . yeah . . . all*
> *right.*

298. C.U. of Joe: 298.

> JOE
>
> *(sleepily)*
>
> *What's up?*

299. C.U. of Chuck: 299.

> CHUCK
>
> *We have to be at a meeting with*
> *this Willoughby guy in half an hour.*

300. C.U. of Joe: 300.

> JOE
>
> *Another pep talk, I guess . . . at*
> *least things are looking up.*

DISSOLVE TO:

301. INT.—HOTEL MEETING ROOM—NIGHT   301.
It is a large room with chairs and a podium, full of mercenary recruits. JOHN WILLOUGHBY, an official of the Rhodesian government, distinguished looking, is addressing the men:

(CONTINUED)

301. (continued)

WILLOUGHBY

. . . and the important thing is that my government thinks it imperative that you men understand the situation. I don't know what you have been told, but you will be facing a determined enemy. Not a bunch of barefoot savages, but a good fighting force with many victories under its collective belt.

(then)

The rebels consider themselves patriots, and therefore have right on their side, to their way of thinking. They are fighting for their homeland, and you are not, which gives them another edge. They operate from passion and conviction . . . and you from a cold, rational, professional point. Historically, mercenaries have not been militarily effective.

302. REACTION SHOT of the men, who are becoming a bit nervous. 302.

303. Back to Willoughby 303.

WILLOUGHBY

(continuing)

You will be effective primarily from a psychological point of view, and you will be relieving regular troops for service in more important areas. This is your last chance to back out,

(CONTINUED)

303. (continued)
> and I would advise those of you
> with any doubts to do so.
>
> *(then)*
>
> Thank you and good luck.

304. C.U. of Joe and Chuck: 304.

JOE
What do you think, Chuck?

CHUCK
What do you mean, what do I think?
Do you have the money to pay them
back? Can you afford to pay for a
round-trip ticket?

305. C.U. of Joe: 305.

JOE
Yeah, I suppose. Besides, at least
Thorton isn't around anymore.

306. C.U. of Chuck: 306.

CHUCK
Don't count on it. I have a feeling
Thorton is like bad luck. Once you
have it, it keeps coming back.

307. L.S. Willoughby walks up the aisle, and Joe stops him. 307.

(CONTINUED)

308. M.S. of Joe and Willoughby: 308.

JOE

Mr. Willoughby, is the picture you painted a pessimistic one or are things really as bad as they seem?

WILLOUGHBY

(looking at name tag)

Mr. Bonner, the picture I painted is an optimistic *one.*

309. C.U. of Joe: 309.

JOE

Optimistic? We were told that the enemy was an undisciplined, unorganized rebel.

310. C.U. of Willoughby: 310.

WILLOUGHBY

Not hardly. Why are you here, Mr. Bonner?

311. C.U. of Joe: 311.

JOE

I ... ah .. need the money and I want *the action.*

312. M.S. of Willoughby: 312.

WILLOUGHBY
Well, my dear Mr. Bonner, that is precisely what you will get.

He turns to leave and then turns back to Joe:

WILLOUGHBY
(continuing)

Joseph, you seem to be an intelligent chap, not like many that we get here. You know, transients, broken men, psychopaths. I offer you some good advice: go home before you open the door to violence and get more than you bargained for. Excuse me and good day.

He leaves and Chuck moves close to Joe.

313. C.U. of Chuck: 313.

CHUCK
What did he have to say?

314. C.U. of Joe: 314.

JOE
(sarcastic)

He told me that I wasn't like the rest of this human flotsam.

He waves his hand toward the other men.

315. C.U. of Chuck: 315.

CHUCK
Maybe he's right.

316. C.U. of Joe: 316.

JOE
*It's too late now . . . Besides, it can't
be that bad.*

> CUT TO:

317. **EXT.—RHODESIAN VELD—DAY**   317.
PANORAMIC SHOT. The sun beats down on a convoy of a
few trucks and jeeps travelling along the highway from
Salisbury to Umtali in the south. The men are cheerful,
and, as the CAMERA ZOOMS IN, we HEAR them TALK and
JOKE.

> DISSOLVE TO:

318. M.S. of the men in the back of the last truck. Joe and 318.
Chuck are with them:

CHUCK
*Joe, when did they say we would
be in Umtali?*

JOE
Sometime tomorrow evening.

319. C.U. of Joe. He lights a cigarette and looks out over 319.
the countryside with obvious pleasure:

JOE

(continuing)

Look at that . . . this country is beau-
tiful. I can see why these people
want to hold on to it. I love these
grasslands.

320. C.U. of Chuck: 320.

CHUCK

When do we get our supplies?

(angry)

They tell us about all the fantastic
equipment we're going to get, and
we leave Salisbury with the clothes
on our backs.

321. C.U. of Joe: 321.

JOE

Stop bitching . . . that's all you do.
What the hell's wrong with you?

322. C.U. of Chuck: 322.

CHUCK

I just don't like it . . .

(pulls Joe close)

(CONTINUED)

322. (continued)

This is serious business, damn it.

> JOE
>
> *What is?*

> CHUCK
>
> *Look at this truck.*

> JOE
>
> *What about it?*

> CHUCK
>
> *Is this the equipment described to us? Is this an armored personnel carrier?*

> JOE
>
> *No. But it's a good truck.*

> CHUCK
>
> *That's not the point ... this is not what it's suppose' to be, and that's not professional. I just hope it's not symptomatic of the whole damn operation down here.*

Joe looks worried now:

> JOE
>
> *I see what you mean.*
>
> *(to himself)*
>
> *If things are less than promised here, close to the capital ... what the hell will we find ...?*

(CONTINUED)

322. (continued)

CHUCK

(nods head)

Yeah ... What will we find in Zulu land?

DISSOLVE TO:

323. EXT.—CAMP—LATE AFTERNOON   323.
As the convoy arrives at the camp, where they stop for the night, the men are met by a sight that was not expected. The camp is worse than they had imagined. The buildings are dilapidated, the grounds are run-down, and the vehicles in which they are to continue on the last leg of the trip to the battle zone are beat-up junk.

324. M.S. of Joe and Chuck, disturbed by the sight of it all: 324.

CHUCK

My God! Look at that.

JOE

What the hell is this? And you were complaining about the other trucks.

CHUCK

Come on.

CAMERA PANS with them to headquarters.

325. INT.—HEADQUARTERS   325.
Joe and Chuck are admitted to see the commander,
who is seated behind his desk with a pile of papers in
front of him:

COMMANDER

(not looking up)

Yes, what is it?

CHUCK

*Sir, we are a little concerned about
conditions here and the vehicles . . .*

COMMANDER

What about them?

Now the commander looks up at them.

326. C.U. of Joe: 326.

JOE

*They don't exactly inspire confi-
dence in this operation.*

327. C.U. of Chuck: 327.

CHUCK

They're falling apart. I think . . .

328. C.U. of the commander, now annoyed: 328.

COMMANDER

*That's what we have to work with
. . . I'm sorry.*

329. C.U. of Joe: 329.

> **JOE**
> *Sir, what we have here is a far cry*
> *from the travelogue we were shown*
> *in the States. Everyone is complain-*
> *ing, sir. We are just the only ones*
> *who have the guts to say anything.*

330. M.S. of the commander. He stands up: 330.

> **COMMANDER**
> *We are far from Salisbury and, as*
> *such, must make do with what we*
> *have . . . and as far as the men are*
> *concerned, our new commander will*
> *have to deal with that . . .*

The door opens behind them:

> **COMMANDER**
> *(continuing)*
> *Ah . . . here he is now.*

331. M.S. of Frank Thorton, as he enters the office.   331.

332. C.U. of Thorton, his cold blue eyes fixing on Joe and   332.
Chuck.

333. C.U. of Joe and Chuck, reacting to the sight of Thor-   333.
ton.

334. L.S. of the four men: 334.

COMMANDER

*Captain Thorton, you will take care
of these men and their complaints,
won't you?*

335. C.U. of Thorton, grinning at Joe and Chuck: 335.

THORTON

*Certainly, commander . . . I will take
good care of these men . . . and I'll
do so personally. And the other
men's complaints, as soon as we
reach Umtali . . .* later.

336. C.U. of the commander: 336.

COMMANDER

That will be all.

They all salute, and Joe and Chuck exit.

337. M.S. of Joe and Chuck. CAMERA MOVES IN: 337.

JOE

*Well, that does it. We're in good
hands now.*

CHUCK

*Yeah . . . only they're around our
throats.*

DISSOLVE TO:

338. EXT.—DIRT ROAD—AFTERNOON   338.
PANORAMIC SHOT. The small convoy of rickety vehicles is strung out on the dirt road; clouds of dust are trailing out behind.

DISSOLVE TO:

339. M.S. of the men in the last truck, where Joe and Chuck 339. are riding. They have handkerchiefs tied over their mouths and noses.

DISSOLVE TO:

340. C.U. of Joe and Chuck, seated in the back of the last 340. truck. They remove their handkerchiefs from their dust-caked faces:

JOE
I bet we can thank our friend Thor-
ton for being stuck at the tail end of
this parade.

341. FAVOR CHUCK. He pulls out a pipe and lights it: 341.

CHUCK
Hey, you're pretty bright.

342. C.U. of Joe, glancing out the open back of the truck: 342.

JOE
Look at that.

343. They have reached the crest of a hill, and a light wind 343.
(CONTINUED)

343. (continued)

blows the dust away. They can see the sunset reflected on the Lampolo river which, like a pink ribbon,
unwinds in the valley below. The convoy stops for a
short break.

344. C.U. of Joe: 344.

JOE

That's beautiful.

345. C.U. of Chuck: 345.

CHUCK

Yes, it is . . . yes, it is.

346. C.U. of Joe: 346.

JOE

*It must have looked just like that to
the first Portuguese who came here
. . . I wonder if they came like we
did.*

347. C.U. of Chuck: 347.

CHUCK

(playfully sarcastic)

By plane? No, I don't think so.

348. C.U. of Joe: 348.

JOE

*No, seriously, I mean, I wonder if
they came for the same reasons.*

349. TWO SHOT: 349.

CHUCK

I don't think so . . .

They are interrupted by Thorton:

THORTON

*Come on, you scum, this ain't no
picnic.*

JOE

Just enjoying the fresh air, Captain.

350. C.U. of Thorton: 350.

THORTON

*You had better. Soon you'll be
smelling Bantu armpits.*

CAMERA PANS with Thorton as he goes back to his jeep.

351. Joe and Chuck frown as they reboard the truck. CAMERA 351.
PANS with the convoy as it descends into the valley.

DISSOLVE TO:

352. L.S. of the convoy, as the base camp, their final des- 352.
tination, comes into view.

DISSOLVE TO:

353. EXT.—CAMP—LATE AFTERNOON   353.

L.S. of the convoy as it comes to a halting stop. CAMERA DOLLIES IN as Joe and Chuck get out of the truck. Finally, the reality of what they have gotten themselves into hits them like the heat of the African sun. CAMERA HOLDS on a CLOSE-UP of Joe and Chuck. They are shocked by what they see.

CUT TO:

354. INT.—BARRACKS   354.

POINT OF VIEW SHOT as the men enter the barracks. The hot sun streams through the broken walls and shattered windows. In the long, dusty shafts of sunlight, stirred here and there by flies and other insects, can be seen rusty cots. Around the barracks, other recruits, like ghosts in the shadows, stare in fear at the newcomers.

355. C.U. of Joe: 355.

JOE

What the hell's this? What's wrong here?

356. C.U. of Chuck: 356.

CHUCK

What's wrong?

(angry)

Do you have eyes, damn it? Look. This place is falling apart. The only men we find here are other recruits— look at their eyes. What are they afraid of?

357. C.U. of Joe: 357.

JOE
*Well, I have a strange feeling it
won't take us long to find out.*

They walk outside.

358. EXT.—CAMP   358.
L.S. of Joe and Chuck as they exit the barracks, de-
scending the steps to the central clearing of the camp.
A couple of shells explode in the clearing, sending
men scurrying for cover. Then there is silence. Thorton
runs by with his two aides, CARTER and RICHARDSON.
Chuck grabs Thorton by the arm.

359. M.S. of the two men: 359.

CHUCK
Thorton.

360. C.U. of Thorton: 360.

THORTON
Captain, soldier . . . it's Captain.

361. M.S. of the men, as Carter sucker punches Chuck in 361.
the face.

362. C.U. of Chuck, lying on the ground.   362.

363. LOW ANGLE SHOT of Thorton, Carter, and Richardson, 363.
standing over Chuck.

364. L.S. of the men, as Chuck scrambles to his feet and 364.
starts to come back at Carter. Both aides reach for
their side arms. Joe holds Chuck back.

365. M.S. of Joe and Chuck. Joe pulls his own pistol and 365.
pretends to side with Thorton, while holding the gun in
the general direction of the three men.

> JOE
>
> *Hey! Calm down ... take it easy,*
> *man. The Captain's right, he's doing*
> *his job.*
>
> (then)
>
> *He's all right, Captain, sir. Just a lit-*
> *tle scared from all the shells, that's*
> *all.*

366. M.S. of the three men. Carter and Richardson move 366.
toward Chuck, but Joe stops them by firing a few
rounds high above their heads.

367. C.U. of Joe: 367.

> JOE
>
> *See? Shooting makes everyone a*
> *bit jumpy. Right?*

368. M.S. of the other recruits, watching. They laugh, and 368.
the crisis is past.

369. M.S. of Carter and Richardson. They lower their guns, 369.
looking at the Captain questioningly.

370. C.U. of Thorton: 370.

THORTON

Okay ... calm down boys.

(to Chuck)

*You just remember, it's Captain. And
don't ever grab my arm again,
soldier, or I'll put a bullet in your
head.*

Thorton and his two aides move off.

371. C.U. of Chuck: 371.

CHUCK

(to himself)

Yeah ... I bet you would.

372. M.S. of Joe and Chuck. Joe pushes Chuck toward the 372.
barracks. CAMERA PANS with them. As they walk, an English recruit, whom we will get to know as BIFF, a power-
ful man in his late forties, comes up to them.

373. C.U. of Biff: 373.

BIFF

You two blokes like a whiskey?

374. C.U. of Chuck: 374.

CHUCK

No.

375. M.S. of the three men: 375.

JOE

Yes, *we would . . . thanks, buddy.*
Joe puts his hand on Chuck's shoulder:

JOE

(continuing)

Come on, we need a drink.

BIFF

We all *need a drink in this place.*

DISSOLVE TO:

376. **INT.—BARRACKS**   376.
L.S. of Joe, Chuck, and Biff as they enter. Once inside
the barracks Biff pulls a bottle out of his gear, along
with two glasses; he pours them a drink and takes a
swig out of the bottle. The few other men who are in
the barracks leave in a hurry.

377. C.U. of Chuck: 377.

CHUCK
What's their problem?

378. C.U. of Biff: 378.

BIFF
You're what's wrong with them, mates. You're poison.

379. C.U. of Joe: 379.

JOE
Because of what happened out there?

380. C.U. of Biff: 380.

BIFF
That's right. You've just signed your death warrants, and they want no part of you, lest they be included.

381. C.U. of Joe: 381.

JOE
What about you?

382. C.U. of Biff: 382.

BIFF
I hate the bloody bastard, and I'm

(CONTINUED)

382. (continued)

> *on the blacklist too ... now there*
> *are three of us.*

He takes another swig and refills their glasses:

BIFF

(continuing)

And them's better odds.

383. M.S. of the three men: 383.
They all smile and drink up, and we—

FADE OUT:

FADE IN:

384. INT.—HEADQUARTERS—MORNING   384.
L.S. The interior, while not luxurious, is far more comfortable than the barracks. In the same building is a
supply store of sorts, the counter of which is close to
the Captain's office. Thorton sits at his desk while the
recruits file into the supply store.

385. L.S. of Joe and Chuck as they enter. A couple of re- 385.
cruits are complaining to the captain, who has left his
desk to investigate the commotion:

1st RECRUIT (o.s.)

... but we were told that ...

386. M.S. of two recruits, talking to Thorton. In the back- 386.
ground Carter and Richardson are lounging, paying
close attention:

(CONTINUED)

386. (continued)

> 1st RECRUIT
>
> *(continuing)*
>
> *. . . all this stuff would be supplied by the organization.*
>
> THORTON
>
> *My aides will take care of any com-plaints you may have.*
>
> *(to his aides)*
>
> *Carter. Richardson. Please take care of these men.*

Thorton returns to his office.

387. M.S. of Joe and Chuck, obviously enjoying the flak that Thorton is catching from the recruits.   387.

388. M.S. of the two aides and recruits: 388.

> 2nd RECRUIT
>
> *Look, we were told that we would be supplied with all the necessary equipment.*
>
> CARTER
>
> *And . . . ?*
>
> 1st RECRUIT
>
> *And now we find out that if we want any of that fancy stuff that sold us to come in the first place, we'll have to pay for it.*

389. C.U. of the 2nd recruit: 389.

2nd RECRUIT
*That's bull, and we won't stand for
it.*

390. C.U. of Richardson: 390.

RICHARDSON
*You will be issued the standard mili-
tary gear ... but if you wish anything extra ...*

391. C.U. of the 1st recruit: 391.

1st RECRUIT
*Wait a minute ... the point is that
we were promised that equipment
... if not, we wouldn't have come,
damn it.*

392. C.U. of Richardson, angry.   392.

393. C.U. of the 2nd recruit: 393.

2nd RECRUIT
*Where are the fancy installations we
were promised? This is a hole.
Where's the hospital? Where ...*

394. M.S. of the four men: 394.

CARTER

*Look, soldier, we told you the story.
Now, if you have any further complaints, let's go into the Captain's office. We don't want to hold up the
whole operation here, do we?*

Carter indicates the door to Thorton's office, and the
four men disappear inside. The recruits cast a look
back at the other men before entering, as though a
doubt had entered their minds.

395. L.S. of Thorton through his door. As the door closes 395.
over the scene, Thorton's eyes stare across the two
rooms and bore into Joe's eyes, almost saying, "This is
for you, Bonner—for you and your friend. Remember
. . . *later?*"

396. C.U. of Joe. His expression tells us that he has re- 396.
ceived Thorton's message.

CUT TO:

397. INT.—MESS HALL—LATE MORNING   397.
M.S. Some men are having coffee. The two recruits,
who had complained to Thorton earlier, come into the
mess.

398. L.S. of the two recruits, walking slowly, their heads 398.
bowed. As they get closer to the other men, silence
pervades. It is obvious that the two recruits have been
beaten savagely.

399. C.U. of Joe and Chuck, who also are having coffee. 399.

400. C.U. of Biff: 400.

> **BIFF**
>
> *That bastard and his goons . . . look*
> *what they've done to these chaps.*

401. L.S. of Biff helping them sit down: 401.

> **BIFF**
>
> *(continuing)*
>
> *That's a bloody shame . . . that's*
> *what it is, a bloody shame.*

402. M.S. of Chuck, rushing over: 402.

> **CHUCK**
>
> *I was a paramedic, let me look at*
> *them.*

403. E.C.U. of Chuck's hands going over the men's faces. 403.
CAMERA FOLLOWS his hands:

> **CHUCK (o.s.)**
>
> *(continuing)*
>
> *Contrary to what usually is done . . .*

404. C.U. of Chuck: 404.

CHUCK
(continuing)
*... these men were only beaten
where it shows.*

405. C.U. of Joe: 405.

JOE
*You think they meant this to be
some kind of example for the rest of
us?*

406. C.U. of Biff: 406.

BIFF
*That's exactly what he means, lad.
After they sell all the supplies,
equipment, and food that they can,
then they'll not care what happens
to us. Then Thorton will sooner kill
you than spit.*

407. C.U. of Chuck: 407.

CHUCK
*They're pretty bad ... they might
even have concussions. That Captain's a hard case.*

408. C.U. of Joe: 408.

JOE
*He's a bad one all right. I wonder
what he's like in action.*

409. M.S. of the men. From his personal supplies, Chuck 409.
puts some gauze bandages on the men:

CHUCK
*Well, I think we'll soon find out. After
that shelling yesterday, it won't be
long before we engage.*

CAMERA PANS with Biff to his pack; he pulls out a whiskey
bottle, takes a swig, and passes it to the injured men.

410. C.U. of Biff: 410.

BIFF
*We better not. We were supposed
to receive training from these blokes
with all that special equipment . . .
and until we do, I'm not going out
there.*

DISSOLVE TO:

411. EXT.—CAMP—AFTERNOON   411.
L.S. The camp is quiet; an air of peacefulness and
calm prevades. CAMERA ZOOMS IN SLOWLY.

DISSOLVE TO:

412. M.S. of the camp. The men are a bit lax in the heat of 412. the afternoon. CAMERA MOVES IN SLOWLY to a small group of men talking in the central clearing. Suddenly, several shells explode and rockets slam into the camp, sending bodies flying and men running for cover. A squad of rebels attack.

CUT TO:

413. INT.—BARRACKS 413.
Joe, Chuck, and Biff respond quickly, picking up their nearby arms, taking positions by the windows.

CUT TO:

414. MONTAGE OF SHOTS 414.
In the central clearing of the camp, and on the periphery, there is havoc. The squad of rebels run through the camp, exchanging gunfire with the recruits who are running for cover. As quickly as the assault began, it ends, without a trace of the rebels.

415. L.S. of Joe, Chuck, and Biff, walking through the 415. smoke and wreckage of the aftermath.

416. M.S. of the men: 416.

JOE
Look at this mess . . . Jesus.

CHUCK
Thank God there weren't too many of them.

417. C.U. of Biff: 417.

BIFF

*They were just teasing, lad ... a
small scouting group ... the same
one that fired those two rounds yesterday. That's why we couldn't find
them ... it's such a small group,
they move too quickly.*

418. C.U. of Chuck: 418.

CHUCK

*You're a recruit, Biff, but you're not
new at this.*

419. C.U. of Biff: 419.

BIFF

*Aye, lad, I'm not new at this. I cut
my teeth in the Congo. The fighting
was worse, but the organization was
better.*

420. L.S. of the men. They return to the barracks; they sit 420.
down on the steps. Chuck lights his pipe.

421. C.U. of Joe: 421.

JOE

Why are you here? White Power?

422. C.U. of Biff: 422.

BIFF

Kill the Zulu? No. I've nothing against these people. They are the patriots . . . Africans.

Then Biff is quiet for a while, staring out at the camp.

423. BIFF'S POV of the camp. It is now early evening, and the 423. last rays of the sun have just disappeared. The fires and lamps have been lighted.

DISSOLVE TO:

424. BACK TO BIFF   424.

BIFF

(continuing)

The ancient name of this country is Zimbabwe, after the ancient city and civilization by the same name. No one knows who built it, but some say that this Zimbabwe was the ancient kingdom of Ophir or King Solomon's mines. It was built before 1100 A.D.

425. CAMERA PANS across the faces of the other men as they 425. listen intently:

BIFF (o.s.)

The Portuguese were the first Euro-

(CONTINUED)

425. (continued)

> *peans to come here in the 16th century.*

426. C.U. of Biff: 426.

BIFF

(continuing)

The Portuguese fought the Nguni, then the Zulu conquered the Nguni. The Zulu fought the British. The Ancient Ruins Company, a bunch of thieves, practically destroyed Zimbabwe, looking for gold. Finally, White Power, backed by British guns, won over the warrior tradition and spears of the Zulu.

(then)

That's why I'm here.

FADE OUT:

FADE IN:

427. EXT.—CAMP—MORNING   427.
L.S. of all the men gathered in the clearing in the middle of the camp. They are standing in formation, waiting for the captain.

428. L.S. of headquarters, as Thorton comes out. CAMERA 428.
PANS with him to the men. He is followed by his aides.

429. C.U. of Thorton: 429.

THORTON

*Yesterday, the rebels attacked this
camp.
Today, we are going to seek them
out and destroy them.*

430. CAMERA PANS across the faces of the men, they seem to 430.
be distraught and begin to MURMUR.

431. M.S. of Thorton: 431.

THORTON

(continuing)

*We will be leaving in an hour, so get
ready, and be in this clearing in
sixty minutes. Get light combat gear,
we have to move fast. Now move.*

432. L.S. of all the men, as they clear out except for Biff 432.
and a few others.

433. C.U. of Carter: 433.

CARTER
Get moving, you scum.

434. L.S. of Biff and the few others, who refuse to move.   434.

435. C.U. of Richardson: 435.

RICHARDSON

*If you don't move, you'll be shot for
refusal to obey orders.*

436. M.S. of Biff and others. The men hesitate, waiting for 436.
Biff, then they move out leaving him standing alone.

437. M.S. of Thorton, as he begins walking toward the Eng- 437.
lishmen, drawing his side arm:

THORTON

*Soldier, I'm only going to say it once
. . . move out.*

438. C.U. of Biff, sweat tracing the furrows of his face: 438.

BIFF

*No, sir. This force is ill-equipped
and unprepared. They have not received the equipment promised, nor
have they received any training . . .
and I'll be damned if I'm going to
have them at my back, and you're a
bloody fool if you do.*

439. M.S. of Thorton, as he quickly raises his hand and 439.
points the .45 automatic at Biff's head.

440. M.S. of Joe, stretching his hand out, running to Biff. 440.
But Chuck grabs him and holds him back:

(CONTINUED)

440. (continued)

JOE

No!

441. TWO SHOT of Thorton and Biff. The shot rips through 441. Biff's head . . . before he has a chance to defend himself. Thorton turns and walks away.

442. M.S. of Joe and Chuck, still struggling: 442.

JOE

You bastard . . . you bloody bastard.

Chuck drags him away before he has a chance to say any more.

443. INT.—BARRACKS 443.
Chuck pushes Joe inside:

JOE

(continuing)

That son of a bitch shot him in the head without batting an eye. I watched him . . . it didn't faze him.

444. M.S. of Joe, as he slams his fist into the wall, tears in 444. his eyes:

JOE

(continuing)

I'm going to kill that bastard.

445. C.U. of Chuck: 445

CHUCK

*And I'll help you. But you have to
wait, bide your time. Then when it's
right, we'll squash him like a bug.*

Chuck slams his hand open-palmed down on a table.

CUT TO:

446. **EXT.—VELD—DAY**   446.

E.C.U., LOW ANGLE of heavy boots and horse hooves
crushing the dry grass. CAMERA PULLS BACK to REVEAL the
mercenaries trekking single file. The commander Thorton and his aides ride horses, while the recruits trudge
on foot.

447. M.S. of Joe and Chuck: 447

JOE

*Where the hell did they get the
horses, and why are we walking?*

CHUCK

*I know they use them for hunting
cattle rustlers when they're not in
the regular army. Thorton keeps
them in the outbuildings some-
where, I guess.*

JOE

*It's the Wyatt Earp syndrome,
Chuck. They're playing cowboys,
and you gotta have a horse.*

448. REVERSE ANGLE behind Joe and Chuck. Chuck gestures 448.
toward the man in front of him:

CHUCK

*Like this clown in front of us. I won-
der how much he paid Thorton for
that special gear.*

Then the first of a series of three gunshots slam into
the man's body, spinning him around, causing him to
fall open-armed into Joe.

449. MONTAGE OF SHOTS   449.
In action, Joe realizes that real violence, cruelty, and
death, stripped of their romantic veneers, are a far cry
from what we see on the screen or what we read in
books. In the battle, most of the recruits are killed immediately. But Joe and Chuck and a handful of others
manage to make it out alive.

450. The small group of men retreat through the tall grass 450.
of the veld.

451. C.U. of Joe: 451.

JOE

Where the hell is Thorton?

452. C.U. of Chuck: 452.

CHUCK

*He's covering his ass . . . he cut out
before we started shooting our way
out.*

453. M.S. of Joe, Chuck, and men: 453.

JOE

*They're all dead, Chuck . . . this is
insane. We didn't know what was
going on.*

(shakes head)

*Crazy . . . all this way, and we get
wiped out after the first engage-
ment.*

1st RECRUIT

What are you going to do now?

454. C.U. of Chuck: 454.

CHUCK

Back to camp.

455. PREVIOUS SHOT   455.

2nd RECRUIT

*Not me, pal, I'm going back to Salis-
bury and back home.*

JOE

*That sounds good to me. What do
you say, Chuck?*

456. C.U. of Chuck: 456.

CHUCK

I said, I'm going back to camp . . .
I'm going to kill him.

457. C.U. of Joe: 457.

JOE

For Christ's sake, Chuck, let it alone.
The other day you told me to wait till
the time was right. Well, it's not. We
have the chance to go now.

458. C.U. of the 1st recruit: 458.

1st RECRUIT

Are you coming with us?

459. M.S. of the men. Joe looks questioningly at Chuck 459.
who, tired of waiting, throws his pipe on the ground:

CHUCK

I'm going to kill that animal.

Then Chuck throws his compass at their feet:

CHUCK

(continuing)

Here, go back. Don't get lost.

JOE

Ah . . . hell, I'm coming.

Joe turns to the others and shakes their hands.

(CONTINUED)

459. (continued)

                    JOE

                (continuing)

    Good luck.

                1st RECRUIT
        Good luck to you, mate.

                            FADE OUT:

FADE IN:

460. **EXT.—VELD—NIGHT**   460.
    The landscape, with its tall grass moving gently in the
    soft evening wind, is illuminated by the pale blue light
    of the moon. Joe and Chuck reach the outskirts of the
    camp undetected.

461. POV SHOT of the camp. From their hiding place, they can 461.
    see the camp clearing. Thorton and his aides are fin-
    ishing loading a jeep with supplies and valuables from
    the dead recruits.

462. C.U. of Joe: 462.

                    JOE
        *Chuck, what's the use? What's the
        sense of it? Chuck . . .*

463. FULL SHOT of Joe and Chuck, crouching low in the tall 463.
    grass. Chuck shrugs off Joe's grasp and rushes into
    the clearing, firing his automatic rifle.

                            (CONTINUED)

464. L.S. of Thorton, Carter, and Richardson at the jeep, as 464.
they are taken by surprise. The two aides go down immediately. Thorton, however, being on the other side of
the jeep, is protected from Chuck's barrage of bullets.
Thorton manages to get off a burst from his own machine gun.

465. L.S. of Chuck as Thorton's rounds rip through his 465.
body, severely wounding him.

466. L.S. of Joe, running from the cover of the trees, firing 466.
his automatic rifle.

467. M.S. of Thorton, taking cover behind the jeep, but not 467.
before dropping his carbine.

468. C.U. of Joe, still running and firing: 468.

JOE
Thorton . . . you son of a bitch . . .
CAMERA TRUCKS with Joe as he runs toward the jeep,
shooting every inch of the way. As he rounds the jeep,
Thorton closes with him, taking the inexperienced man
by surprise. The force of Thorton's attack knocks the
rifle out of Joe's hands. Thorton thrashes at Joe with a
bayonet.

469. E.C.U. of Joe's hand reaching for his own bayonet.   469.

470. PREVIOUS SHOT   470.
Thorton pushes Joe back, bending him over the jeep.

471. C.U. of Thorton: 471.

THORTON
*You should have gone home, boy
... at least you could have died in
bed.
Now you're going to die in the dirt.*

472. M.S. of Thorton and Joe. Thorton stabs down at Joe, 472.
misses, getting the blade stuck between two sections
of metal in the jeep. As he struggles to free the blade,
Joe lunges up with his bayonet, sending the blade into
Thorton's ribs up to the hilt. Joe screams; he throws
Thorton's body off himself and down to the ground.
Joe can hear the rebels approaching the camp now.

473. FULL SHOT of Thorton's corpse, face down in the dirt.   473.

474. L.S. of Joe. CAMERA TRUCKS with him as he staggers 474.
back to Chuck and drags his unconscious form into
the bush.

475. EXT.—VELD—NIGHT   475.
In the background we HEAR the rebels DESTROYING the
camp, as Joe struggles with Chuck to put as much
distance as possible between them and the rebels. As
they work their way back to the capital:

CHUCK
What did you do with Thorton?

(CONTINUED)

475. (continued)

JOE

I killed him.

CHUCK

· *Good ... good ... I'm dying, Joe.*

476. C.U. of Joe: 476.

JOE

*You wanted it, damn it. Why didn't
you come away when we wanted
to? Damn it. Why did you have to
come back here? For what? An
ideal? A cause? That's bull, man,
bull. That's a waste, man; we're
going to die for nothing.*

477. C.U. of Chuck: 477.

CHUCK

We did what we thought was right.

478. L.S. of Joe and Chuck, stopping to rest. Joe eases 478.
Chuck down in the tall grass:

JOE

*I know, that's the point ... we were
wrong. It's pathological, Chuck. We
were sick ... we were suffering
from a terrible disease ... emotional
boredom. We know that we had to
dedicate ourselves to something.
The thing we should've dedicated*

(CONTINUED)

478. (continued)

> *ourselves to was life, not death . . .*
> *and that's what it was, Chuck . . . a*
> *death wish.*

479. M.S. of Chuck, as he looks up at Joe: 479.

CHUCK

Give me a cigarette, Joe.

480. PREVIOUS SHOT   480.

Joe lights a cigarette. CAMERA TILTS DOWN with him as he kneels and places the cigarette in Chuck's mouth. CAMERA MOVES IN:

CHUCK

(continuing)

It's strange how strong man clings to life, no matter how willing he seems to throw it away.

JOE

For the wrong things, Chuck. You didn't come back to do anything necessary. We should've gone back home.

481. C.U. of Chuck: 481.

CHUCK

Come on, Joe . . . we shouldn't have come here in the first place. Things weren't that bad after all, were they,

(CONTINUED)

481. (continued)

> *Joe? That beer cellar near Hog's Head. Ah . . . I wish I had my stereo here, Joe, and some of that dark beer. We could play "The Charge of the Light Brigade" . . .*

Chuck starts humming the music:

CHUCK

(continuing)

What were we looking for?

482. C.U. of Joe: 482.

JOE

We were looking for something to justify our useless lives. We weren't looking for anything. We were trying to lose ourselves.

483. POV SHOT as a dog sneaks into their hiding place, cow- 483. ering on its belly closer and closer.

484. M.S. of Chuck: 484.

CHUCK

Look at that . . . he's lonely and comes to us. Get lost, mutt, we're losers.

The dog nuzzles up to Chuck and lies next to him. Chuck pets him.

(CONTINUED)

484. (continued)

                    CHUCK

                 (continuing)

    *That's one of the greatest feelings to
    have: a dog asleep next to you in
    front of a fire.*

485. C.U. of Joe: 485.

                     JOE

    *That's what I'm talking about. Those
    are the important things. We had to
    come to Africa to find that out.
    When we get back, we'll enjoy
    those things again, Chuck. We'll
    raise hell again.*

Joe starts to breakdown:

                     JOE

                 (continuing)

    *Man, we'll enjoy it all, Chuck . . .
    Chuck? Chuck?*

CAMERA PANS as Joe looks over at Chuck. Chuck's head
is now slumped to the side and the cigarette falls from
his mouth, while the dog licks his bloody hand:

                     JOE

                 (continuing)

    *Chuck, don't leave me alone . . .
    Jesus. Don't leave me alone.*

                            DISSOLVE TO:

486. L.S. of Joe burying Chuck as best as he can in the tall 486. grass. As a heavy rain begins to fall, Joe, while crying, lifts his head and screams into the night, raising his fists to the heavens. CAMERA SLOWLY PULLS BACK silhouetting Joe against the night sky.

FADE OUT:

FADE IN:

487. EXT.—VELD—DAWN   487.
Joe pushes on. After some narrow escapes when Joe comes close to rebel forces, he comes up to a deserted plantation house. The heavy rainfall continues.

488. POV SHOT of the plantation house.   488.

489. PREVIOUS SHOT   489.
Joe moves toward the house, where he hopes to find shelter from the elements.

DISSOLVE TO:

490. INT.—PLANTATION HOUSE   490.
L.S. In the dark shambles of the interior, which was obviously once a home of luxury, Joe sees that the house is empty. CAMERA TRUCKS with him into the library, which is almost intact; the volumes are now ruined by the rains coming in through the broken ceiling.

491. M.S. of Joe, looking at the volumes; he turns around, 491. startled.

492. M.S. of a LONE REBEL.   492.

493. C.U. of Joe, looking around quickly to see if anyone 493.
     else is present. CAMERA PANS QUICKLY around the library.

494. M.S. of Joe, as he points his rifle at the rebel.   494.
     Joe can see that the rebel has taken shelter in the
     house from the storm. Now Joe has the advantage, for
     he is armed with several automatic weapons, while the
     rebel has only a knife:

                         JOE
          *I don't want trouble . . . just get out
          of here . . . go.*

495. C.U. of the rebel, who is scared, just staring at Joe.   495.

496. M.S. of Joe: 496.

                         JOE
                     (continuing)
          Hell, you don't understand me.

497. C.U. of the rebel: 497.

                        REBEL
                     (in Bantu)
          Why did you come here?

498. C.U. of Joe: 498.

JOE

*I don't understand you. I don't mean
you any harm . . . just go.*

499. C.U. of the rebel: 499.

REBEL

*You wish to kill me, like you have
done to all my people . . . but we
will kick you into your grave.*

500. M.S. of Joe and the rebel: 500.

JOE

*I don't understand . . . get out of
here. Get your gear and go.*

Joe points to a bundle of things on the floor with the
muzzle of his rifle, at which time the rebel lunges at
him with his knife. The force of the blow carries the
rebel over the muzzle of the rifle, which goes off acci-
dentally.

501. M.S. of Joe, as his face and hands are splashed with 501.
blood, which steams hot in the cool morning air. Joe
moves to the rebel's bundle and goes through its content. He finds a battered book. He opens it and sees
the title.

502. E.C.U. of the book's title page, which reads, *Vol de* 502.
Nuit, a novel by Antoine de Saint-Exupéry.

503. C.U. of Joe. The sight of the book touches him, be- 503.
cause he had read the book in college and for the first
time he starts to understand it.

504. FLASHBACK of Joe's college PROFESSOR lecturing about the 504.
book:

PROFESSOR

*. . . danger and near death had
given him an appreciation of the
simple things, a real love of life . . .*

CUT TO:

505. EXT.—VELD—NIGHT   505.
MONTAGE OF SHOTS, Joe working his way back to Salisbury and safety.

DISSOLVE TO:

506. INT.—WILLOUGHBY'S OFFICE—DAY   506.
L.S. of Willoughby standing behind his desk, talking on
the phone. Joe sits in a leather chair opposite the man.
Joe has been cleaned and fed. As Willoughby talks
into the phone, the CAMERA MOVES IN:

WILLOUGHBY

(into the phone)

*. . . yes, Joe Bonner, the sole sur-
vivor of the Lampolo group of mercenaries . . . that's right . . . immediately. Is that understood?*

(hangs up)

(CONTINUED)

506. (continued)

> *Mr. Bonner, from a grateful govern-*
> *ment, you will receive full pay and*
> *passage home to the States.*

507. M.S. of Joe, as he stands up, almost in a daze: 507.

JOE

> *You have to stop these recruiters*
> *... someone should do something.*
> *(takes Willoughby's hand, shakes it)*
>
> *Thank you.*

After shaking hands, a SECRETARY comes in and escorts
Joe out.

DISSOLVE TO:

508. INT.—SHIP'S CABIN—EARLY EVENING   508.

> Joe sits in the cabin, writing a wire to Mary back
> home.

509. E.C.U. of the wire.   509.

510. PREVIOUS SHOT   510.

> As we SEE Joe leave the cabin, we HEAR the end of the
> WIRE:

Joe (V.O.)

> *... and as I stood at the rail watch-*
> *ing ...*

511. EXT.—SHIP'S DECK—EARLY EVENING   511.
    Joe stands at the rail watching the setting sun.

512. L.S. of the setting sun sinking into the ocean. African 512.
    wild geese fly silhouetted against its redness:

JOE

(continuing)

... the wild geese flying overhead on their Night Flight, I thought of my Night Flight, which had brought me here and would take me home, and I realized that courage, real courage, is in fighting the peaceful battles of everyday existence.

THE END

Chapter **6**

STORYBOARDING

"A picture is worth a thousand words."

This bit of wisdom by an ancient Chinese philosopher aptly expresses the importance of the storyboard. As we have already seen, the purpose of the script is to previsualize the film as concretely and exactly as possible. How better to do this for a visual medium than with pictures?

By sketching the shots, we are able to see or show exactly what we want the film to look like. We can, in a sense, view the film before it is recorded by the camera. By sketching the shots, however rough, we are able to see:

1. How the shots are composed.

2. How the shots are cut (edited) from one shot to the next.

3. How the film flows.

The very last form in the script's evolution is the storyboard. This last step is usually ignored by books on scriptwriting. This is an oversight because scripting and storyboarding belong together. By storyboarding your script as you write, you can make corrections for mistakes in continuity that you might not catch otherwise.

As we have already mentioned, the writer's involvement generally ends with the screenplay or master scene script. But for the total filmmaker who is involved in all phases of production (including writing a shooting script), a look at storyboarding will be useful in visualizing how a film's shots work together. Even for the writer who is not concerned with creating a shooting script, storyboarding can be a great help in stimulating ideas when making the transition from a film's treatment to its master scene script, as pointed out in Chapter 4.

Figure 6-1

L.S. LOW ANGLE JOE:

In the case of a storyboard based on a treatment, the script is not divided by shots but rather by scenes. The scenes have to begin with a particular image and the storyboard helps to transfer this image from the mind to the paper. Anyone who doubts this has only to consider film director Alfred Hitchcock, whose beginnings were in a motion picture studio's

Figure 6-2

art department doing storyboards, and whose work eventually became a kind of odyssey from "cerebral cinema"—a planned movie consisting only of mental images—full circle to a complete storyboard drawn from the shooting script.

One does not have to be an artist to do storyboards. Stick figures are acceptable, even in the professional film industry.

Details are not needed. The only thing one must do in the picture is duplicate as closely as possible the camera position and camera angle needed for the real shot.

Figure 6-3

The storyboard is drawn for the director (and ideally, by the director), so that the cinematographer knows how the shots are to be composed. This aids in the shooting process and cuts down on the set-up time.

The shots taken from the shooting script are sketched out on paper and placed on the production office wall in their proper order, giving us a good idea of how the film flows.

As we have said, the important thing to remember is to duplicate the camera position and camera angle at the moment of cutting to the following shot. For static shots this is relatively easy.

The task of storyboarding becomes more difficult when the shot to be sketched is a moving shot, such as PANS, TILTS, etc. These can be done well if we take care to sketch the crucial points of the camera movement.

These crucial points will include: (1) the beginning of the PAN, (2) any important objects that we want to cover in the PAN, (3) the end of the PAN, or (4) the end of the shot before the next transition. The storyboard should contain the sketch along with notes on the camera position, the camera angle, the shot number, and a brief description of the action.

Figure 6-4

In the film industry, storyboarding is often used for very difficult sequences, such as shots which cannot be repeated for the camera. These are the kinds of shots that have to be worked out to the smallest detail, starting first on paper to avoid mistakes that would waste time—time, as we have said before, which is money.

Figure 6-5

Some directors—such as Steven Spielberg and Alfred Hitchcock—use storyboarding extensively, to the point of storyboarding the entire script. Storyboarding is a tremendous aid to the filmmaker and should be used by the director and writer alike.

An excellent example of fine storyboarding is to be found in comic books of the realistic, non-cartoon type. One good exercise that helps to improve storyboarding skills is to cut out

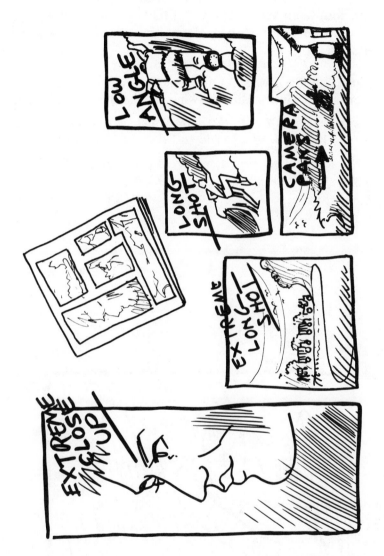

Figure 6-6

the frames of these comic books, mount them on sheets of paper, and write camera positions and camera angles for them.

In the following examples we illustrate the three points which sum up the importance of the storyboard. The storyboard tells us:

1. *How shots are composed.* As an example, we choose shot #437: Thorton walks toward Biff, drawing his sidearm (Figure 6-7).

2. *How shots cut from one to the next.* We show the cut from shot #437 to #438: *M.S. of Thorton* to *C.U. of Biff* (Figure 6-8).

3. *How the film flows.* We show the whole "killing of Biff" sequence (Figure 6-9).

Figure 6-7

#437

M.S. THORTON

CUT TO:

#438

Figure 6-8

C.U. BIFF

Figure 6-9

We close with the opening shot, #1, of the shooting script. Storyboard some of the subsequent shots yourself. Remember that the artistic quality of the drawings is of no importance. Good luck.

Figure 6-10

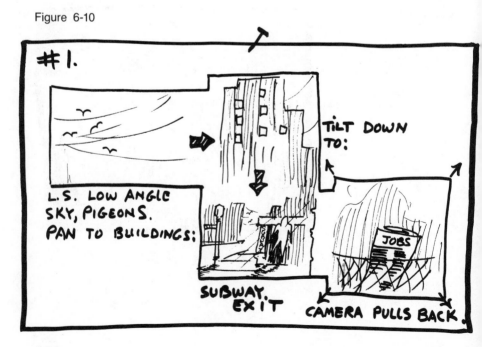

Index

Action:
 added to outline, 12
 in script, 32
Avant-garde cinema, 2, 4

Camera, 106
Camera movement, illustration, 109
 shown in storyboards, 237
Cerebral cinema, 1
Characters, 7
 creation in outline, 11
Cinema:
 avant-garde, 2, 4
 cerebral, 1
Close Encounters of the Third Kind, 4
Concept, 4-5
 development into outline, 9
 sample, 5-6

Descriptive material, in script, 29
Devices, 7
Dialogue, 7, 31, 32
 in treatment, 20
 types of, illustration, 110

Fellini (Federico), 2, 3, 4.
 Voyage of G. Mastorna, The, film project, 3

Hitchcock, Alfred, 3, 235, 238

Locations, 7
 creation in outline, 11
 in script, 29-31

Master scenes, 31
Master scene script (screenplay), 4, 29-32
 sample, 33-104

Night Flight:
 concept, 5-6
 outline, 14-16
 treatment, 23-27
 master scene script, 33-104
 shooting script, 115-232

Outline, 7-13
 amplifying of, 8
 characters, creation in, 11
 locations, creation in, 11
 rough, 10-11
 second draft, 12-13
 sample, 14-16

Previsualization, 1-2, 233
Production, script's importance to, 2-3

Scenic heading, 29, 106
Screenplay (master scene script), 29-32
 (*see also* Script)
Script:
 "blueprint of the film," 3
 financing, as basis for, 1-2
 importance to production, 2-3
 ironclad, 3
 locations in, 29-31
 loose, 4
 master scene (screenplay), 4, 29-32
 registering with Writer's Guild of
  America, 8
 samples, 33-104, 115-232
 shooting, 105-13
Shots, 4, 106-7
 illustration, 108
 in storyboards, 233
 in treatment, 21
Spielberg, Steven, 3, 238
Storyboarding, 4, 233-42
 to stimulate script ideas, 234
Storyboards:
 camera movements in, 237
 quality of art, 236
 shots in, 233

Transitions, 112-13
 illustration, 111
Treatment, 17-21
 dialogue in, 20
 length, 18
 saleability, 18
 sample, 23-27
 shots in, 21
 visual imagery in, 18-19, 20

Visual and audio symbols, 7
Visual imagery in treatment, 18-19, 20
Vol de Nuit (Antoine de Saint-Exupéry),
  12, 13, 16, 27, 102, 228
Voyage of G. Mastorna, The (Fellini film
  project), 3

Writer's Guild of America, 8